Baker & Spice

exceptional cakes

Dan Lepard &
Richard Whittington

Quadrille

Publishing director Jane O'Shea
Creative director Helen Lewis
Project editor Janet Illsley
Art director Mary Evans
Food for photography Dan Lepard
Stylist Róisin Nield
Design Paul Welti
Design Assistant Katherine Case
Production Bridget Fish

First published in 2007 by
Quadrille Publishing Limited
Alhambra House
27-31 Charing Cross Road
London WC2H 0LS
www.quadrille.co.uk

Text © 1999 Richard Whittington
and Dan Lepard

Recipe photography © 1999 Peter Williams

Location photography © 1999
Emily Andersen

Design and layout © 2007
Quadrille Publishing Limited

Cataloguing in Publication Data:
a catalogue record for this book is available
from the British Library

ISBN-13: 978 184400 4522

Printed in China

Contents

"What makes a cake special are the quality of the ingredients, their generosity and their freshness, not elaborate decoration. Our cakes are essentially simple constructions that are complete when they come from the oven. They are closer to good home baking than classic French pâtisserie, with its complex creams, additives and custards."

DORIT MEINZER, PASTRY COOK

Introduction

Baker & Spice's extraordinary and beautiful original shop that once sat so prettily in London's smart Walton Street started its life as a window for Gail Stephens' existing trade-baking business. It was only gradually, as the Victorian ovens were restarted and on-site production began for the local community, that it took shape and flourished, developing the unique identity that has made it famous. Other shops have since opened, in Belgravia, Queen's Park and Maida Vale.

With a cult following across London and beyond, Baker & Spice is the most successful boutique-style food retailer in the country. When you visit the shops, first impressions are overwhelming. This is the bakery and pâtissierie of your dreams and those dreams were probably set in Paris, not London. As you admire the stacks of beautiful breads and trays of pastries giving off their sweet, alluring smells – all of them hand-made by bakers working on the premises and using traditional ingredients and methods – it is hard to believe that the roots of such excellence were in vans, not stone ovens, in a delivery service for bread baked by other people, for customers too small for the big bakers to be bothered with. Today's shining star in British artisanal baking has its roots in an innovative and successful service operation, which allowed Gail Stephens to set up the shop that has become so famous.

"We are what we buy and that has moral as well as price consequences." she says. "We use as much that is organic as possible. We work with the seasons and are very careful about where our raw materials come from. Does it have to travel half way round the world to get here? If something comes from the Third World, who exploited whom to get it here? I don't sit in the office and buy blind on the telephone. I go to Covent Garden market daily, and read and check every label on every box of fresh produce that I buy. I smell and feel the goods as well as taste them. Once a month I go to a big dried fruit, nut and spice importer. Buying is never on auto-pilot. I really spend a lot of time with suppliers to get it right."

"Everything we sell is baked on the premises. What you see is what you get and what you get is what we make. And that involves learned technique and very hard work. The whole point of Baker & Spice is that it is self-contained; we don't buy in anything ready-made. We do things the way people used to do them, which in the age of factory farming and supermarkets have largely been forgotten". Practically, that means seven 18-hour working days in every week.

"Changes occur in what is baked in some sense by natural progression, but also by listening to the customers. Partly because of that we have become a real village shop. We are the neighbourhood.

We reflect it and it reflects us." Baker & Spice is remarkable in its consistency, which is the direct consequence of the calibre of the staff. Those who work here are part of a team and they share the same commitment to quality, achieved in an ethical environment.

CAKES

There is a tradition of thoughtful home cake making – the skillful mixing of fine ingredients, combined by hand and baked in small batches – which has found continued professional expression at Baker & Spice. This is the legacy left to the business by Dorit Meinzer and it represents the very best home baking tradition from around the world.

Mass-produced cakes tend to be very basic, but are dressed up after they are baked to make them look more special than they really are. This is quite the opposite of the Baker & Spice approach, where there is little or no decoration of the cakes after they cool from the oven. Here everything is in the making. Thus the final flavour in every Bramley apple and Calvados cake is achieved before the cakes are baked. There is no icing to camouflage and no decoration to distract from poor texture and flavour. What is achieved is the result of the best ingredients and careful baking techniques, nothing more and nothing less.

PASTRIES AND BRIOCHES

'Viennoiserie' describes the highly specialised area of croissant and puff pastry making, something in which Baker & Spice excels. Patrick Lozach was the man who first created the croissants, the brioche and fine butter pastries for the shop. Trained in Brittany over 20 years ago, his work reflects the traditions of 'old school' French baking, before the additives and colours of the chemical industry took hold of the small pâtisseries. As with the bread at Baker & Spice, the source of the ingredients for the Viennoiserie plays an important part in the quality Patrick was able to achieve. The doughs are mixed using French 'T550', a slow-milled low-extraction wheat flour that gives a crisp texture to the exterior of the croissants and to baguettes. The flour's low gluten content holds the layers intact and separate, through repeated turning and folding, creating a tender melting crumb and a crisp short finish to the crust.

Much of the cheaper Viennoiserie sold in Britain, and increasingly in France, contains an orange-dyed butter, a mixture of milk fat from EC countries, reprocessed and packaged as 'French butter'. The croissants at Baker & Spice are made exclusively with L'Escure, an appellation controllé unsalted French butter. L'Escure is not used because it is from France, but because it is the best butter there is. The pain au chocolat is filled with Belgian Callibaut Couverture – a fine high-cocoa-content chocolate with a strong bittersweet taste. The almond croissants are filled with ground almonds, sugar, butter and egg yolks. No artificial flavours, no essences, no bulking agents, just lots of almonds and fresh butter.

BAKING AT HOME

Exceptional cakes enables you to recreate many of the cakes, pastries and other sweet baked goods on offer at Baker & Spice through recipes which, while detailed, communicate simply how to get the best results. All the recipes have been tested in a domestic kitchen using non-professional electric and gas ovens.

Everything that is done in the bakery to maximise the efficiency of production carries through usefully into the practice of the domestic baker. Whether creating classic light sponge cakes or learning how to layer pastry with air and butter to produce beautifully crisp and light mille feuilles, this is the most practical of kitchen handbooks. It is not about the hard work of a professional baker, but a story of finding and giving pleasure through the making of delicious things for everyday enjoyment at home.

"If bread is the staff of life, then cakes, pastries, biscuits, scones and meringues are part of baking's pleasure principle."

Essentials

Breadmaking is traditionally a separate activity within bakeries that also produce cakes, pastries and biscuits, demanding different skills and time frames. This is the case at Baker & Spice, where different teams work in each area. But the bringing together in the shop of everything that is made expresses the totality of baking as a specialised cooking discipline and, in the range of techniques, tastes and textures on display, a happy reflection of the home baking experience.

OVENS AND EQUIPMENT

All the recipes in this book have been tested in standard but
contemporary gas and electric ovens without convection (ie not fan
assisted). Before starting to bake, invest in an oven thermometer and
check your oven's accuracy. You may be in for a surprise. Even brand
new and expensive ovens carry no guarantees that they will achieve the
exact temperature designated by each setting.

If your oven is more than a few degrees above or below the correct
temperature you need to get it checked by an engineer. Usually the
cause is a faulty thermostat or it may be that the oven has been wrongly
calibrated. If the oven is brand new, you should have no difficulty in
having this rectified. Even if it is out of its guarantee period, there are
specialist companies that repair and maintain ovens. A more difficult
problem to overcome with an underperforming gas cooker is gas
pressure. Contact your gas supplier if this turns out to be the cause of an
oven not achieving high temperatures.

As all keen cooks know, you never seem to have too much
cooking equipment and there is always a use for another bowl, whisk
or sieve. For baking you must have accurate scales. A powerful table-
top electric mixer is another great asset. Wherever possible, we have
suggested the minimum rather than the maximum requirements.

must haves:

measuring jugs and spoons

scales – digital is best

table-top electric mixer with beater
or paddle, whisk and dough
hook attachments

hand balloon whisks

food processor

mixing bowls in different sizes

wooden spoons, numerous

wooden board for shaping

plastic and rubber spatulas

palette knife

scissors

rolling pin

rimless metal baking sheet

linen cloths and tea towels

oven thermometer

several heavy baking trays

non-stick Swiss roll tins

loaf tins, 500g and 1kg

cake tins in different sizes, both round
and square

springform cake tins in different sizes

tart tins with detachable bases (large
and individual)

pastry cutters

piping bag and tubes

steel ruler

silicone mat or non-stick baking
parchment

pastry brush

skewer for testing cakes

wire cooling rack

optional, but helpful:

calculator

digital timer

flour dredger

deep-frying/sugar thermometer

marble rolling sheet

large and small brioche moulds

"Small changes in the balance of ingredients can make big changes in the finished cake. There are no revolutions – things are made better very gradually, a natural process that takes time. This is the same as at home when a recipe is cooked over and over, with little changes and refinements each time."

Cakes

Virtually all cakes are made from soft, low-gluten flour, butter, eggs and sugar, their respective proportions and the method of their incorporation defining the texture of the cake when it is baked. After that, what makes each cake individual is a matter of shape, the flavourings used, and how it is iced, filled and decorated. The relative proportions of the base ingredients also determine the most appropriate cake-making technique.

A high percentage of butter points to 'creaming' at the outset, where the butter is vigorously whipped or whisked with sugar until it becomes pale and absorbs air from the beating action, the air being the element that ensures a light texture when the cake is baked. A cake made with lots of eggs – a classic sponge – begins by whisking them with sugar, and results in a baked finish that literally springs back when gently pressed. Cakes with high levels of treacle, honey or chocolate start with these being warmed or melted, thereby making it possible to integrate them with the other primary ingredients.

Cake batters are raised using chemicals rather than yeast. The most common raising agents are bicarbonate of soda – which is sometimes referred to as baking soda – and baking powder, of which bicarbonate of soda is the main active ingredient. Chemical raising agents only generate gas briefly, which is why they are unsuitable for lifting breads that need a sustained and lengthy leavening. It is the difference in gluten levels between hard or strong (bread) flours and soft (cake) flours which makes bread and cake texturally so different.

When bicarbonate of soda, an alkali, is mixed with an acid, a chemical reaction is kick-started and carbon dioxide is given off. Bicarbonate of soda can therefore only be used on its own to lift a batter if a suitable natural acid is present. This might be something like lactic acid, which is contained in yoghurt and buttermilk, or citric acid or vinegar.

Baking powder is a complete raising agent that only needs water to make it work. It consists of a mixture of bicarbonate of soda and acid salts, with ground starch included to absorb moisture from the air. It is this inert 'buffer' of starch that prevents premature activation in the tin in humid conditions.

Baking powder contains two different types of water-soluble salt crystals that are triggered sequentially. The first, typically cream of tartar, reacts with moisture at room temperature and initiates a reaction with the bicarbonate of soda, instantly giving off little bubbles of carbon dioxide. A second acid salt crystal, usually sodium aluminium sulphate, activates only at high temperature, in the oven,

generating a larger amount of carbon dioxide. The moist solids of the cake batter dry during cooking and set round the bubbles before the gas generation stops, producing a light yet moist cake.

Self-raising flour includes sufficient baking powder to raise most cakes and scones. However, over years of making cakes at Baker & Spice we have found that many are improved texturally by adding a little bicarbonate of soda or baking powder with the self-raising flour. There is always a trade-off in such experiments, though – add too much and it will leave a bitter chemical taint in the mouth. The cake will also have a tough crumb. Different brands of self-raising flour contain different amounts of raising agent. The suggested additional raising agent must therefore be treated as a guide and not an absolute.

The combination of chocolate and pecan nuts in this cake is pleasing and not overly sweet. The cake is rich and buttery, however, and a small slice satisfies.

Chocolate pecan cake

MAKES A 23CM CAKE

180g good-quality bittersweet
   chocolate, chopped
180g unsalted butter + extra
   for the tin
4 eggs, separated
140g caster sugar
225g pecan nuts, ground
100g plain flour, sifted

ICING

360g good-quality bittersweet
   chocolate, chopped
250g unsalted butter
2 tbsp golden syrup

DECORATION

50g white chocolate, chopped

Preheat the oven to 180°C, Gas 4. Butter a 23cm springform cake tin. Line the bottom with a disc of non-stick baking parchment.

Melt the chocolate and butter in a heavy-based pan over a low heat, then set aside to cool. Put the egg yolks and two-thirds of the sugar in the bowl of a heavy-duty electric mixer fitted with the whisk and beat until thick and light in colour. In another bowl, whisk the egg whites with the remaining sugar until they hold a soft peak. Fold the melted chocolate into the whisked egg yolks, then fold in the ground pecans and flour. Finally, fold in the whisked egg whites.

Pour the cake mixture into the prepared tin. Bake in the centre of the oven for 45–50 minutes or until a skewer inserted in the centre of the cake comes out with a few slightly sticky crumbs clinging to it. Transfer to a wire rack and leave to cool completely in the tin.

To make the icing, warm the chocolate, butter and golden syrup in a heavy-based pan over a low heat until smoothly combined. Remove from the heat and leave to cool to a thick, pouring consistency.

Remove cake from tin and place on a rack over a tray. Pour on the icing, spreading it gently over the top and sides with a palette knife.

For the decoration, melt the white chocolate in a bowl set over a pan of just simmering water. Put into a small greaseproof paper piping bag (or a small polythene bag), snip off the tip and pipe in random lines over the icing on the top of the cake. Draw a skewer through the piped white icing to make squiggles. Leave to set before serving.

Coffee cake with mascarpone cream

MAKES A 20CM CAKE

225g self-raising flour
2 tsp baking powder
225g caster sugar
225ml corn oil
2 eggs, separated
4 tsp coffee extract, or 2 heaped tsp
    instant coffee granules dissolved in
    2 tsp boiling water
75ml full-fat milk
butter for the tin

ICING

250g mascarpone
$1/4$ tsp grated lemon zest
350g icing sugar, sifted
2 tbsp strong espresso, or 2 heaped
    tsp instant espresso dissolved in
    2 tbsp boiling water

Preheat the oven to 180°C, Gas 4. Butter two 20cm springform cake tins and line the bases with discs of non-stick baking parchment.

Sift the flour, baking powder and caster sugar into a mixing bowl. Beat in the oil, egg yolks, coffee and milk. In a second bowl, whisk the egg whites to soft peaks.

Stir a spoonful of the whites into the cake mixture before gently folding the rest through. Divide the mixture equally between the prepared tins. Bake for about 45 minutes or until the sponges spring back when gently pressed in the centre. Transfer to a wire rack to cool, unmoulding the cakes while still warm and leaving them on the rack to cool completely.

For the mascarpone icing, put the mascarpone and lemon zest in a bowl and mix together with a spoon. Slowly add the icing sugar, about one-third at a time, working each addition in completely with the spoon before adding the next until you have a thick paste. Finally, beat in the coffee, a spoonful at a time, until completely incorporated.

Spread half the icing on one sponge, then put the second sponge on top. Smooth the remainder of the icing over the top of the cake using a palette knife.

Lemon cake

ILLUSTRATED ON PREVIOUS PAGES

MAKES I SMALL LOAF CAKE

115g self-raising flour
I tsp baking powder
2 eggs
115g caster sugar
65ml double cream
grated zest of I lemon
I tbsp lemon juice

45g unsalted butter, melted
melted butter and flour for the tin

ICING

30g icing sugar
I tsp lemon juice

Preheat the oven to 170°C, Gas 3. Lightly grease a 500g loaf tin with melted butter. Line the bottom with a buttered rectangle of non-stick baking parchment, then dust the paper and sides of the tin with flour.

Sift together the flour and baking powder. Lightly beat the eggs with the sugar until just combined. Beat the cream into the eggs for a minute, then add the lemon zest and juice. Fold in the flour until lightly combined, then gently and carefully fold in the melted butter.

Pour the mixture into the loaf tin. Set the tin on a baking tray in the middle of the oven and bake for 45 minutes or until a skewer inserted in the centre of the cake comes out clean. Leave to cool in the tin for 10 minutes, then run a knife between the cake and the sides of the tin. Very gently upturn the cake on to your cloth-covered hand, then place the cake upright on a wire rack to finish cooling.

For the icing, sift the icing sugar into a bowl and slowly stir in two-thirds of the lemon juice until combined. Add more lemon juice to make a slightly thin icing, but don't thin it too much – the icing will thin further when left for 2–3 minutes. Brush the icing over the top of the cake, letting it drip a little down the sides.

Light yet full of flavour, this is a fresh-tasting sponge cake with an appealing and strong citrus colour.

Apricot cake

MAKES A 23CM CAKE

200g unsalted butter,
    softened
350g caster sugar
3 eggs
225g self-raising flour
150g sour cream

12 apricots, halved and stoned
melted butter and flour for the tin

TO FINISH
45g caster sugar

Preheat the oven to 170°C, Gas 3. Lightly grease a 23cm springform cake tin with melted butter. Line the bottom with a disc of non-stick baking parchment and butter it, then dust the paper and the side of the tin with a little flour.

In a heavy-duty electric mixer, cream the butter with the sugar until light and fluffy. Slowly beat in the eggs, one at a time, until well combined. Fold a third of the flour into the butter and egg mixture, followed by a third of the sour cream, then repeat. Finally, fold in the remaining flour and sour cream.

Spoon the mixture into the prepared cake tin. Lay the fruit on the surface, cut side up, leaning each apricot half slightly on to the next in concentric circles to cover the top completely. Finish by sprinkling with the extra sugar. Bake in the centre of the oven for 50 minutes or until a skewer inserted in the centre of the cake comes out clean.

Leave to cool in the tin for 10 minutes, then run a knife between the cake and the side of the tin. Release the spring-lock on the side of the tin, remove the collar and leave the cake to cool completely on a wire rack before serving.

A rich batter produces a classic sponge, the apricots on the top nestling in the cake which rises up around them as it bakes. Semi-ripe, firm plums can be used instead of apricots.

Carrot cake

MAKES A 23CM CAKE

300g self-raising flour
¹/₄ tsp baking powder
¹/₄ tsp bicarbonate of soda
I tsp ground cinnamon
¹/₂ tsp ground cloves
¹/₄ tsp grated nutmeg
pinch of fine Maldon salt
4 eggs
335ml sunflower oil
450g caster sugar

I25g grated carrots
I40g chopped walnuts
2 tbsp hot bottled spring water
melted butter and flour for the tin

ICING

I30g unsalted butter, softened
300g full-fat soft cheese (Philadelphia),
   softened
I60g icing sugar, sifted

Preheat the oven to 180°C, Gas 4. Lightly grease two 23cm spring-form cake tins with melted butter. Line the bottom of each tin with a disc of non-stick baking parchment. Butter the paper, then dust the paper and the side of the tins with a little flour.

Sift together the flour, baking powder, bicarbonate of soda, spices and salt. Separate two of the eggs.

Using an electric mixer, beat together the oil and sugar. Slowly add the whole eggs, mixing well, then beat in the 2 egg yolks. Beat in the grated carrots, then stir in the chopped walnuts. Using a large metal spoon, fold in the sifted flour mix followed by the hot water.

In another bowl, whisk the 2 egg whites until soft peaks form. Carefully fold them into the cake mixture.

Divide the mixture between the prepared tins and set them on a baking tray. Bake in the middle of the oven for 45 minutes or until a skewer inserted into the centre comes out clean. Leave to cool in the tins for 10 minutes, then carefully release the cakes from the tins and leave to cool on a wire rack.

To make the icing, beat all the ingredients together to a smooth, thick cream. With a palette knife, spread a layer of icing on one cake, then press the other on top. Spread the rest of the icing over the top and side of the cake, swirling it attractively. Chill for at least 2 hours before cutting, and keep the cake in the fridge until ready to serve.

Carrot cake is unusual, both in its use of a root vegetable and in the use of oil for the fat content. Cinnamon is the predominant flavour, moderated by back notes of nutmeg and cloves – the overall sweetness of the cake nicely balanced by the highly aromatic spicing. The grated carrot lends an exceptionally moist texture.

Honey and spice cake

MAKES I LARGE LOAF CAKE

3cm piece of fresh root ginger, peeled
125g runny honey
50g golden syrup
140g unsalted butter
50g dark soft brown sugar
2 eggs

40g rye flour
100g self-raising flour
$1/2$ tsp baking powder
$1/2$ tsp ground cinnamon
$1/2$ tsp ground allspice

Grate the ginger on to a double thickness of muslin and squeeze the ginger in the muslin over a bowl, to extract as much juice as you can. Discard the ginger pulp. Reserve the juice.

Preheat the oven to 170°C, Gas 3. Line the bottom and sides of a 1kg loaf tin with non-stick baking parchment.

In a saucepan over a low heat, warm the honey, golden syrup, butter and brown sugar until hot and the butter is almost melted. Transfer the mixture to the bowl of a heavy-duty electric mixer fitted with the whisk. Beat for $2^1/2$ minutes at medium speed, then add the eggs and ginger juice and continue beating for another $2^1/2$ minutes. The mixture will have cooled, lightened and thickened appreciably.

Sift together the flours, baking powder and ground spices, then sift a second time. Fold the dry ingredients into the honey mixture using a spatula. The mixture will be unusually wet. Pour it into the prepared tin and set on a baking tray in the centre of the oven. Bake for 50–60 minutes or until the top of the cake is a dark golden brown and it feels spongy, springing back lightly when gently pressed.

Transfer to a wire rack and leave to cool to room temperature in the tin before unmoulding.

This loaf cake has a light and airy texture. A little fresh ginger juice spikes the mixture, underpinning the more aromatic ground spices with its clean, hot taste.

Marble cake

MAKES I LARGE LOAF CAKE

100g good-quality bittersweet
chocolate, chopped
125ml milk
120g unsalted butter, softened
170g caster sugar

2 eggs
225g self-raising flour
I tsp baking powder
65g sour cream
butter and flour for the tin

Preheat the oven to 170°C, Gas 3. Lightly grease a 1kg loaf tin with melted butter. Cut a rectangle of non-stick baking parchment to fit the bottom of the tin and put it in place. Butter the paper, then dust the paper and the inside of the tin with a little flour.

Put the chocolate and 50ml of the milk in a bowl and set over a pan of gently simmering water to melt. Remove from the heat.

Using a heavy-duty electric mixer, cream the butter with the sugar until light in colour and fluffy in texture. Slowly beat in the eggs, one at a time, until well combined. Sift the flour with the baking powder. Mix together the sour cream and remaining milk. Fold one-third of the flour into the butter and egg mixture, followed by one-third of the sour cream mixture. Fold another third of the flour into the mixture, again with one-third of the sour cream. Fold in the remaining flour and sour cream. Spoon half of the mixture into another bowl. Add the chocolate mixture to one half and fold in.

Spoon the two mixtures alternately into the prepared tin, to give a marbled effect. Set the tin on a baking tray in the middle of the oven and bake for 50–55 minutes or until a skewer inserted in the centre of the cake comes out clean.

Leave to cool in the tin for 10 minutes, then gently turn out and place upright on a wire rack to finish cooling.

Swirling the chocolate through the batter gives the cake its distinctive appearance when cut, and hence the name.

Chocolate génoise royale

ILLUSTRATED ON PREVIOUS PAGES

MAKES A 23CM CAKE

GENOISE
60g unsalted butter + extra for the tin
4 eggs
115g caster sugar
115g plain flour
60g cocoa powder

CHOCOLATE MOUSSE
150g caster sugar
3 eggs, separated + 3 egg yolks
1 tbsp cocoa powder

200ml whipping cream
100g unsalted butter, diced
250g good-quality bittersweet
chocolate, chopped
1 tbsp brandy

DECORATION
75g good-quality bittersweet
chocolate, chopped
cocoa powder for dusting

Preheat the oven to 170°C, Gas 3. Butter a 23cm springform cake tin. Line the bottom with a disc of non-stick baking parchment.

Make the génoise: melt the butter in a pan over a low heat, then remove and leave to cool. Put the eggs and sugar into the bowl of a heavy-duty electric mixer fitted with the whisk and beat at a medium speed for 6–10 minutes until the mixture rises. It is very important to incorporate as much air as possible at this stage to ensure a light result. Continue to beat until you achieve a ribbon consistency (1), when the mixture will be quite stiff and an off-white, cream colour.

Remove the bowl from the mixer. Sift the flour and cocoa and add to the bowl. Incorporate by stirring gently (2, 3). Pour in the melted butter and, using a rubber spatula, starting from the centre at the base and working outwards and upwards, fold the mixture over while rotating the bowl one quarter turn (4). Repeat three more times, which means you will have turned the bowl one complete revolution after completing the fourth fold. This is the best way of mixing all the ingredients thoroughly without losing too much air by being heavy-handed – if you overwork the mixture at this point you will end up with a flat and heavy cake.

continued overleaf...

Pour the mixture into the cake tin and bake on the middle oven shelf for 20 minutes. Then, quickly open the oven door and insert a skewer into the centre to test whether the cake is done. If it comes out clean then it is ready. If sticky crumbs adhere to it, give it another 5 minutes baking and test again. It might still need 5 more minutes. When satisfied it is cooked, remove to a wire rack to cool.

Unmould the cake when it is cool and carefully slice off the risen centre to give a flat surface. Wash and dry the springform tin. Cut a strip of non-stick baking parchment to fit around the inside of the tin. Put the prepared génoise back in and reserve.

To make the chocolate mousse, put 50g of the sugar, the 6 egg yolks, cocoa powder and the cream in a bowl set over a pan of simmering water. Stir with a wooden spoon until hot, or the mixture thickens sufficiently to coat the back of the spoon. Remove from the heat and gradually beat in the butter and chocolate until melted and fully combined. Stir in the brandy. Whisk the egg whites with the remaining sugar to soft peaks, then fold them into the mixture.

Pour the mousse mixture on top of the génoise base in the tin. Cover and refrigerate for 4 hours or overnight before unmoulding.

When ready to serve, unmould carefully by sliding a warm palette knife around the inside of the tin before unclipping the side. Leave the cake on the tin base.

For the decoration, melt the chocolate in a bowl set over a pan of just simmering water. Pour on to a clean, dry metal tray and spread out thinly. As the chocolate cools, test it every so often – you want to catch it before it sets hard. When the chocolate is firm enough to work with, shave off large curls using a palette knife. Transfer the curls carefully to the top of the cake, piling them up. Finish with a dusting of cocoa powder.

For a plain génoise simply omit the cocoa powder. A slice of plain génoise with ripe seasonal berries or a summer fruit coulis makes a light and elegant dessert.

Génoise cakes are made by a French technique, which those brought up making Victoria sponges initially find tricky. However, an electric mixer helps you achieve a consistent light result easily. Génoise sponges are best baked the day before they are needed as they will slice better. In fact, they can be well wrapped in cling film and refrigerated for up to 3 days, or they may be frozen for up to 2 weeks.

If ever a génoise comes out rather dry, prick the surface deeply with a needle all over and spoon on some rum or brandy, then leave for 12 hours before serving. This very rich chocolate mousse génoise is based on a recipe developed by our first pastry chef, Henri Berthaux. It makes a fine dessert cake.

Devil's food cake

ILLUSTRATED ON PREVIOUS PAGES

MAKES A 23CM CAKE

150g good-quality bittersweet
   chocolate, chopped
115g caster sugar
125ml milk
40g cocoa powder
3 eggs, separated + 1 egg yolk
150g unsalted butter, softened
   + extra for the tin
85g muscovado sugar
225g plain flour
1 tsp Maldon salt, ground fine
1 tsp bicarbonate of soda
170g sour cream

ICING

200g good-quality bittersweet
   chocolate, chopped
60g cocoa powder
100ml bottled spring water
1 tbsp golden syrup
45g unsalted butter, softened
280g icing sugar, sifted
2 egg yolks

Preheat the oven to 170°C, Gas 3. Lightly butter two 23cm spring-form cake tins and line the bottom of each one with a disc of non-stick baking parchment.

Make the cake: put the chocolate, caster sugar, milk, cocoa powder and 2 egg yolks in a bowl set over a pan of simmering water. Stir to make a coherent custard-like mixture. Remove from the pan of water and reserve.

Using a heavy-duty electric mixer, beat the butter with the muscovado sugar until light and fluffy. Beat in the remaining 2 egg yolks, then the flour, salt and bicarbonate of soda. Fold in the sour cream followed by the chocolate mixture. In another bowl, whisk the egg whites until they hold peaks, then fold through the cake mixture until combined.

Divide the mixture between the prepared tins and lightly smooth the top. Bake in the centre of the oven for 45–50 minutes or until a skewer inserted into a cake comes out clean. Place on a wire rack and leave to cool completely in the tins.

To make the icing, put the chocolate in a bowl and set over a pan of simmering water to melt. In a pan over a low heat, warm the cocoa powder, water and golden syrup until hot but not boiling. Add the melted chocolate and whisk until combined. Remove from the heat and beat in the butter, icing sugar and egg yolks until smooth and creamy. Taste and add a little more sugar if liked. Leave to cool until the icing is thick but spreadable.

Remove the cakes from the tins and cut each into two layers. Sandwich the four layers together, spreading a little icing between them, and finish by thickly spreading icing over the top and side of the cake, with a palette knife. Leave in a cool place overnight to firm, but not in the fridge which would make the icing go dull.

Cakes bearing this rather provocative title, with all its implications of wicked excess, are often disappointing, typically being too sweet and not chocolatey enough. Our version has an unusually large amount of melted chocolate, both in the sponge and in the icing, to strike the right indulgent note. It is one of Dorit Meinzer's delectable creations.

Yeast cakes are a feature of German
baking, and this one is filled typically
with a walnut and chocolate mixture.
It could also have a more spicy,
Middle Eastern filling that includes
poppy seeds.

Krantz cake

MAKES 2 CAKES

1 sachet fast-action yeast
500g strong white flour
1 tbsp warm bottled spring water
150g cream cheese
150g sour cream
150g caster sugar
150g unsalted butter, melted
4 egg yolks
pinch of Maldon salt, ground fine
sunflower oil for the bowl and tins

FILLING

100g caster sugar
100g walnuts
100g good-quality plain chocolate,
    roughly chopped

GLAZE

1 egg yolk, beaten with 1 tbsp milk
50g caster sugar
50ml bottled spring water

In a bowl, mix the yeast with 2 tbsp of the flour and the water. Cover and leave in a warm place for 2 hours or until it starts to bubble.

Whisk together the cream cheese, sour cream, sugar, melted butter and egg yolks, using an electric whisk, then add the yeast batter and remaining flour. Beat on a medium speed for 5–6 minutes, adding the salt as the mixture combines. Transfer the sticky dough to a lightly oiled bowl, cover with cling film and leave in the fridge overnight.

The next day, remove the dough from the fridge 20–30 minutes before you start working with it. Oil two 500g loaf tins. For the filling, whiz the sugar and walnuts in a food processor to a fine crumb. Tip into a bowl and mix in the chocolate.

On a lightly floured surface, roll out the dough to a rectangle 4mm thick. Spread with the filling and roll up like a Swiss roll, from a long side. With a sharp knife, halve the roll lengthways, then twist the two pieces together loosely, keeping the cut sides up. Cut the loaf across in half. Drop each piece into a prepared loaf tin, cover and leave to rise in a warm place for 1$\frac{1}{2}$–2 hours. Preheat the oven to 180°C, Gas 4.

Brush the egg mix over the cakes and bake for 15 minutes. Lower the setting to 160°C, Gas 3 and bake for a further 25–30 minutes until well coloured. Dissolve the sugar in the water and bring to the boil. Brush over the cakes while still hot, then leave to cool in the tins for 10 minutes, before turning out on to a wire rack to cool completely.

Chocolate and hazelnut brownies

ILLUSTRATED ON PREVIOUS PAGES

MAKES 16 SQUARE BROWNIES

120g unsalted butter, softened
250g caster sugar
2 eggs + 1 egg yolk
210g good-quality bittersweet
    chocolate, melted
4 tbsp espresso coffee, cooled

1 tbsp rum or brandy
165g plain flour
1 tsp baking powder
$^1/_4$ tsp Maldon salt, ground fine
30g whole hazelnuts
icing sugar for sprinkling

Preheat the oven to 180°C, Gas 4. Line the bottom and sides of a 23cm square tin that is 5cm deep with foil.

Cream the butter and sugar together in a bowl. Slowly add the eggs, one at a time, and then the yolk, mixing well after each addition. Stir in the melted chocolate, then the coffee and the rum (or brandy). Sift the flour, baking powder and salt together, and gently fold into the chocolate mix.

Pour the mixture into the tin and lightly press the hazelnuts over the surface. Bake in the middle of the oven for 20–25 minutes or until a skewer inserted near the centre comes out warm at the tip, with slightly sticky crumbs clinging to it. (Avoid overcooking, or you'll end up with a dry sponge. It is safer to err on the side of underdone.)

Leave to cool in the tin before cutting into squares. Dust the brownies with icing sugar to serve.

Chocolate brownies probably owe their popularity to their rich, moist interior. To ensure the right consistency, the batter should be worked gently — beating hard will incorporate too much air, delivering a spongy finish.

Orange cheesecake brownies

ILLUSTRATED ON PAGES 46–7

MAKES 16 SQUARE BROWNIES

340g full-fat soft cheese, softened
100g caster sugar
1 egg yolk
30g plain flour
grated zest of 1 orange

1 tbsp freshly squeezed
    orange juice
1 recipe Chocolate brownie mixture
    (see opposite)

Preheat the oven to 180°C, Gas 4. Line the bottom and sides of a 23cm square tin that is 5cm deep with foil.

Cream together the soft cheese and sugar. Add the egg yolk, then the flour. Finally mix in the orange zest and juice. It is important that the consistency be quite thick: achieving a similar texture between the cheese and the chocolate brownie mixtures is the intention. Put the cheese mixture into a piping bag fitted with a 1cm nozzle.

Spoon half of the brownie mixture into the tin. Pipe half of the cheese over the top, moving from one side to another in swirling bands, pushing the cheese into the chocolate mixture as you do so. Spoon on half of the remaining brownie mixture, then pipe over the remaining cheese, pushing it into the chocolate as before. Finish by spooning on the last of the chocolate. Take a skewer and zig-zag the swirls to accentuate the effect.

Bake as for chocolate and hazelnut brownies (opposite). Leave to cool in the tin, then cut into squares to serve.

A rippled effect is achieved by swirling a soft, sweetened, orangey cheese mixture between layers of sticky chocolate. The contrast of flavour and texture is very appealing.

Blueberry bran muffins

MAKES 18 MUFFINS

100g bran
300ml milk
300g self-raising white flour
2 tsp bicarbonate of soda
1 tsp baking powder
3 eggs

160g caster sugar
85g muscovado sugar
300ml sunflower oil + extra for
    the tray
200g blueberries, washed and left
    to dry

Preheat the oven to 170°C, Gas 3. Lightly oil a 12-cup muffin tray or
line with paper muffin cases.

Mix the bran and milk together. Leave aside until you have mixed
the other ingredients. Sift the flour, bicarbonate of soda and baking
powder together. In a large bowl, lightly beat the eggs with the sugars
and oil. Fold in the sifted flour, then lightly fold in the soaked bran
and milk. Finally, add the fruit and fold lightly to combine. Do not
overmix – there should still be some traces of flour evident.

Spoon the mixture into the muffin cups to fill almost to the top.
Bake in the centre of the oven for 20–25 minutes. Leave to cool until
warm, then eat immediately.

When baked, muffins should have a firm texture, unlike a
sponge, the top well risen and golden brown. Often the
crown splits slightly which is how it should be. Eat the
muffins while they are still warm from the oven – they are
never as nice when completely cold.

"Our meringues have always been a favourite with regular customers, particularly with children whose eyes light up at the sheer scale of the treat. People are surprised by the size and the intensity of the whiteness. They are literally the first display you see when you step through the door."

Meringues, Scones etc

Some of our most popular sweet items at Baker & Spice don't fit neatly into 'cakes', 'pastries' or 'biscuits', though they certainly merit inclusion in this book, so we have combined them in this short section. Meringues, scones and doughnuts have long been a central part of afternoon tea.

Meringues

ILLUSTRATED ON PREVIOUS PAGES

MAKES 12 MERINGUES
115g egg whites
225g caster sugar
30g flaked almonds

Preheat the oven to 150°C, Gas 2. Cover 2 large baking trays with non-stick baking parchment or a silicone mat.

Put the egg whites and sugar in a bowl set over a pan of simmering water, and stir until the sugar has dissolved and the mixture is quite warm to the touch. Transfer the mixture to the metal bowl of a heavy-duty electric mixer and beat with the whisk attachment until thick and cool – about 15 minutes.

Spoon 6 large mounds of meringue on to each tray and lightly sprinkle with the almonds. Place the baking trays in the oven and immediately turn the oven setting down to 120°C/Gas $^1/_2$. Cook for 45 minutes. Turn off the heat and leave the meringues to cool completely in the oven before removing. If you have a gas oven with a pilot light, you can turn the oven off when you put the tray in and leave the meringues to dry out overnight.

Serve whole meringues with a fruit coulis, vanilla or chocolate ice-cream, whipped cream, Greek yoghurt and, seasonal berries Or, toss berries with kirsch and sugar, mix with whipped cream and crushed meringues, and then freeze as a parfait. Or, ripple pieces of meringue through ice-cream by adding them in the last few minutes of churning.

Our meringues are sweet, crisp, big – about 10cm across –
and as light as air. They are delicious eaten on their own.
The difference in texture between our meringues and
others comes from warming the egg whites and sugar over
hot water before prolonged whisking, during which the
meringue cools as it stiffens. The professional baker always
uses egg whites by weight for accuracy.

meringues, scones etc

Scones

MAKES 16 SCONES

450g self-raising white flour + extra
  for dusting
pinch of Maldon salt, ground fine
25g caster sugar + extra for sprinkling
2 tsp baking powder
85g unsalted butter, softened
2 eggs

200ml cold milk
85g sultanas (optional)

GLAZE

1 egg yolk
1 tbsp milk

Preheat the oven to 170°C, Gas 3. Line a large baking tray with non-stick baking parchment. Sift the flour, salt, sugar and baking powder into a bowl. Add the butter and rub in with your fingertips. Lightly beat the eggs, add the milk, then pour into the flour. Mix quickly and lightly together, adding the sultanas if you wish. Don't overwork the dough – the quicker and lighter you are, the better the scones will be.

Tip the dough on to a lightly floured surface and roll out to a 2.5cm thickness. With an 8cm cutter, cut out 16 rounds and place 5cm apart on the prepared baking tray. Lightly beat the egg yolk with the milk for the glaze. Brush over the tops of the scones, then sprinkle with a little sugar. Bake in the centre of the oven for 20–25 minutes or until risen and lightly browned.

Cool on a wire rack, then split and fill with jam and cream.

The secret of a good moist, light scone is the correct proportion of raising agent to flour. Use too much leavening and your scone will stand tall, but taste horribly of baking powder. You also need to keep handling to a minimum, otherwise the gluten in the flour is overworked, making the dough elastic and the scone hard.

Doughnuts

ILLUSTRATED ON PREVIOUS PAGES

MAKES 20 DOUGHNUTS

1 sachet fast-action yeast
175ml warm milk (about 20°C)
170g plain white flour
280g strong white flour + extra for
    dusting
1 tsp Maldon salt, ground fine
85g unsalted butter, diced and
    softened

2 eggs, beaten
85g caster sugar + extra for coating
grated zest of 1 lemon
1 tsp ground cinnamon
sunflower oil for brushing
oil for deep-frying

Make the sponge: in a large bowl, whisk together the yeast and the warm milk until the yeast has dissolved. Stir in the plain flour. Cover the bowl with cling film and leave in a warm place for 2 hours or until the sponge has risen by at least one-third and is clearly active, with lots of bubbles.

Put the strong flour in the bowl of a heavy-duty electric mixer fitted with the dough hook and add the sponge and salt. Turn on at the lowest speed. Add the butter one piece at a time. When fully incorporated, add the beaten eggs, one at a time. Add the sugar, grated lemon zest and cinnamon, and knead for 8 minutes. Turn to full speed and knead for a further 2 minutes.

Turn the sticky dough out on to a heavily floured surface and finish kneading by hand, incorporating additional flour until you have a smooth, elastic ball of dough. Brush this with a little oil and place in a lightly oiled bowl. Cover with cling film. Leave to prove at room temperature for 2 hours or until at least doubled in size.

Turn the dough on to the floured surface and gently press out to a rectangle. Divide into 20 equal pieces, rolling them into balls. If you want to make ring doughnuts, make a hole in the centre of each ball by pushing your finger through, then circle your finger to enlarge the hole to about 2cm in diameter. Put the doughnuts on a floured tray and cover with a cloth. Leave to rise in a warm place for 40–50 minutes or until doubled in size.

Heat the oil for deep-frying to 190°C. Fry the doughnuts in small batches, being careful not to overcrowd the pan as this will cause the temperature of the oil to drop below sealing point. Deep-fry for 1–2 minutes on the first side, then turn and give them a further minute on the other side. When done, drain on kitchen paper.

Put some caster sugar on a plate and turn the doughnuts in this to coat while still warm. Serve as soon as possible – they are best eaten as soon as possible.

The two keys to successful doughnuts are a properly proved sweet yeast dough and clean oil at the right temperature. Any neutral-tasting oil, like sunflower, will do. At the correct temperature (190°C), the exterior of the doughnut is sealed, preventing excessive fat absorption, and the carbon dioxide gas trapped inside the dough expands rapidly, giving the right, airy light texture. Frying a yeasted dough gives a completely different exterior finish to baking and a lovely, uniform golden brown colour.

Our sweet fritters are made by mixing chopped seasonal fruit into a fairly thick batter and deep-frying them. As the dough is quite wet, it moulds round the fruit easily.

Plum fritters

300ml warm bottled spring water (about 20°C)

1 sachet fast-action yeast

125g plain white flour

170g strong white flour

15g caster sugar + extra for dredging

grated zest of 1 lemon

1 tsp Maldon salt, ground fine

4 ripe plums

oil for deep-frying

Put the warm water in the bowl of a heavy-duty electric mixer fitted with the dough hook. Add the yeast and switch on at low speed, then add all the remaining ingredients except the plums. Work for 10 minutes to produce a shiny, thick batter. Alternatively, make the batter using a hand whisk. Cover the top of the bowl with cling film and leave to prove in a warm place for 2 hours.

Heat oil for deep-frying to 190°C. Cut the plums in half and discard the stones. Add the plums to the batter and fold them in.

Using a large metal spoon, scoop out one batter-coated plum half and lower it gently into the hot oil. Add another 3 batter-coated plums to the pan, keeping them separate, then deep-fry for 4–5 minutes, turning the fritters over halfway through. They will expand and set and turn golden brown.

Remove with a spider or slotted spoon to kitchen paper to drain. Dredge with caster sugar and serve as soon as possible, frying the remaining fritters in small batches.

Ripe Victoria plums make great fritters, although they can be made using a variety of fruit – really anything that is not too wet. Fritters are best enjoyed still warm – and certainly never more than 2 hours after frying.

Prune clafoutis

SERVES 6

400g stoned prunes, preferably
    Agen prunes
50ml brandy
50g caster sugar

BATTER

125g plain flour
150ml full-fat milk
50ml double cream
30g unsalted butter
2 eggs
50g caster sugar
butter and flour for the baking dish

If using prunes that need to be rehydrated, put to soak overnight in an infusion of weak, sugared tea. Drain, then put back in the bowl, add the brandy and sugar, and toss to coat evenly. Leave to macerate for 2–3 hours at room temperature.

Preheat the oven to 180°C, Gas 4. Grease a 30 x 20cm baking dish with butter, then dust lightly with flour and reserve.

To make the batter, sift the flour into a bowl. In a pan, heat the milk and cream together until hot but not boiling. Remove from the heat and add the butter, then leave it to melt.

With a hand-held electric mixer or whisk, beat the eggs and sugar together until pale and creamy, then add the milk mixture. Stir in gently with a spoon. Fold in the flour to make a smooth, soft batter. Do not beat hard as this would toughen the cooked mixture and affect the rise.

Drain the prunes and distribute them evenly in the prepared dish. Pour over the batter. Bake for 40–45 minutes or until the batter has risen up around the prunes and the surface has a nice golden colour.

Clafoutis originates from Limousin in central France and traditionally features the tiny black cherries the region is famous for. It can also be made with halved fresh plums or apricots. Prunes, enlivened with a little brandy and sugar, make a particularly good clafoutis, especially Agen prunes. If preferred, the clafoutis batter can be baked in a sweet pastry case (page 102) to make a different tart that is delicious served with whipped cream.

"Biscuits and cookies are delicious fripperies, which at their most delicate, can please a discerning palate. In their sugary and more accessible forms they've given pleasure to children and the young-at-heart since medieval times, sweet mouthfuls that crunch appealingly and then burst with candied flavour on the tongue."

Biscuits and Cookies

Biscuits to the British are cookies to Americans, and both terms describe a huge variety of sweet or sometimes savoury bites that are usually – but not invariably – small, crisp discs or wafers. They may be lightly leavened – a small sponge can sometimes be a biscuit – and their texture can be soft, or chewy like toffee, or snapping-crisp.

Biscuits may be either sweet with sugar or honey or, by contrast, be salty or flavoured with cheese or anchovies. Chocolate biscuits can be dry with just a hint of chocolate or moist, spongy and intensely chocolate flavoured. Rich biscuits are shortened with masses of butter, while a water biscuit makes a dry and austere partner for cheese. Dried fruit can outweigh the crumb in a recipe, but it does not stop the end result from being called a biscuit. Shortbreads are biscuits too, as are fig rolls, Garibaldis, cream crackers, rusks, cheese straws, ginger nuts, chocolate chip cookies, sugar-crusted langues-de-chat and almond tuiles.

The first biscuits were not unlike the first breads, crude and coarse flat cakes bound with water and cooked on a hot griddle. Oat cakes were probably one of the first biscuits ever made. With the wider availability of wheat, simple water and flour biscuits became standard fare for travellers. Slow-baked twice to eliminate all moisture, this was the hard tack which sustained the early sailors, so hard it had to be soaked in water before it could be chewed. It also had to be tough enough to resist infestation by insects, at least for several months – after a year at sea, ship's biscuits seethed with weevils.

The first biscuits baked for culinary pleasure were served after medieval banquets and often literally contained sweetened fish and meats along with the sugar and spices that proclaimed a person's wealth and generosity to the world.

By the 1600s sweet biscuits were widely eaten in well-to-do households, typically little pieces of sweet pastry coated with sugar icing, though not all biscuits were sweet. The Bath Oliver was the eighteenth century invention of a certain Dr Oliver of Bath who claimed great digestive properties for them. He encouraged his society patients to eat them as a remedy to counter the effects of their meat-rich diet, an eighteenth-century pointer towards a later scientific understanding of balanced diet and nutrition.

Biscuits gradually developed national or cultural characteristics which are still identifiable today. Thin wafers perfumed with rose or orange water and studded with slivered nuts are popular in the Middle

East and North Africa, while rye and poppy seed crispbreads are very Scandinavian. American cookies still celebrate New World ingredients such as chocolate, pecan nuts and molasses. Biscuits based on a stiff dough that can be cut in any shape often have attachments to religious festivals, some dating back to a pre-Christian era. One thinks of gingerbread men and the German Christmas *springerle* – glazed biscuits with animal figures representing the Nativity, which are punched from a specially embossed rolling pin.

Shortbread

AMAKES 16 BARS OR WEDGES

150g unsalted butter + extra
    for the tin
225g plain flour
4 tbsp cornflour
1/2 tsp baking powder

125g caster sugar + extra for
    sprinkling (optional)
1/4 tsp Maldon salt, ground fine
1 tsp vanilla essence (optional)

Lightly butter a 24 x 20cm Swiss roll tin (or two 16cm fluted tart tins).

Dice the butter straight from the fridge and put into a mixing bowl to soften for about 30 minutes. Sift the flour, cornflour and baking powder on top, then add the sugar, salt and vanilla essence, if using. Rub together gently between your fingertips and, as the mixture coheres, form it into a ball. (Alternatively, put the sifted dry ingredients in the bowl of a heavy-duty electric mixer fitted with the whisk. Add the diced butter, then mix at low speed until the butter and flour have combined and the mixture resembles breadcrumbs.)

For bars, gently pack the mixture into the prepared Swiss roll tin. Mark the surface into bars with a knife, lightly cutting lengthways in half and then across. Prick the top all over with a fork.

For traditional shortbread rounds, shake some caster sugar on to a work surface. Cut the dough in half and shape into two balls on the sugared surface. Put each ball into a tart tin and gently press out into an even layer, making it slightly thicker at the edges and crimping between finger and thumb. Prick the surface all over with a fork and make 4 bisecting shallow cuts from edge to edge like the spokes of a wheel (so the shortbread can be divided neatly into 8 equal wedges when baked).

Refrigerate for 30 minutes to 1 hour before baking. Preheat the oven to 180°C, Gas 4. Bake the shortbread for 18–20 minutes, when the surface will be slightly coloured and just firm to the touch. Leave in the tins until completely cooled before removing.

Benedict bar

ILLUSTRATED ON PAGES 72–3

MAKES 16 BARS

100g unsalted butter, + extra for
the tin
60g caster sugar
1 tsp vanilla essence

200g flaked almonds
3 tbsp milk
1 recipe shortbread dough (opposite)
raspberry jam

Preheat the oven to 180°C, Gas 4. Lightly butter a 24 x 20cm Swiss roll tin.

Put the butter, sugar, vanilla essence, almonds and milk in a small, heavy-based saucepan over the lowest heat, and warm until the butter has melted. Remove from the heat and leave until cool.

Press the shortbread dough into the tin. Spread a thin layer of jam over the surface, then spread the topping mixture over the jam. Bake as for shortbread (opposite), allowing 25–30 minutes.

Shortbread lends itself to rich toppings. The one above is reminiscent of Bakewell tart and takes its name from the South African Benedict cake, which has similar flavours. Plain shortbread bars (left) are great topped with caramel and chocolate (like the filling for the tart on page 109). Pour the caramel mixture over the baked shortbread in its tin and leave to cool and set. Finish with the chocolate topping, then refrigerate before cutting into neat bars.

biscuits and cookies

Date shortbread bars

MAKES 16 BARS

250g dates
grated zest of 1 orange
25g unsalted butter + extra for the tin

1 tsp ground cinnamon
200ml bottled spring water
1 recipe shortbread dough (page 74)

Preheat the oven to 180°C, Gas 4. Lightly butter a 24 x 20cm Swiss roll tin.

Put the dates, orange zest, butter, cinnamon and water in a pan and bring to the boil. Remove from the heat and leave to cool before putting the mixture in a food processor. Pulse-chop to a coarse paste and use at once.

Press two-thirds of the shortbread dough into the tin. Spread the date topping mixture over the surface. Sprinkle the remaining shortbread dough on top like a crumble. Bake for 25–30 minutes. Leave to cool in the tin.

Chewy, sweet and aromatic, the date filling with its citrus tang of orange and smoky cinnamon contrasts nicely with the crisp and buttery biscuit.

biscuits and cookies

Oatmeal and raisin cookies

ILLUSTRATED ON PREVIOUS PAGES

MAKES 20 COOKIES

115g unsalted butter, softened
100g light soft brown sugar
115g caster sugar
1 egg, lightly beaten
4 tbsp bottled spring water

2 tsp vanilla essence
100g self-raising flour
1 tsp Maldon salt, ground fine
250g rolled oats
100g sultanas

Preheat the oven to 180°C, Gas 4. Line two baking trays with non-stick baking parchment.

Using a heavy-duty electric mixer, cream the butter with the sugars until light and fluffy. Gradually add the egg, beating until evenly combined. Then beat in the water and vanilla essence before folding in the remaining ingredients.

Roll the dough into walnut-sized pieces between your palms and put them on the prepared baking trays, leaving space between the cookies to allow for expansion as they cook. Bake for 15 minutes or until firm but still with some give to the gentle press of a finger. Leave on the trays for a few minutes to firm up, then transfer to a wire rack and allow to cool completely.

Moist, sweet and definitely more-ish, these oatmeal and raisin cookies are enjoyed by adults and children alike. For a more sophisticated flavour, soak the raisins in brandy for a couple of hours before incorporating them in the dough.

Chocolate biscuits

MAKES 20–30 BISCUITS

110g plain flour
30g cocoa powder
1 tsp bicarbonate of soda
1/2 tsp Maldon salt, ground fine
115g good-quality bittersweet
   chocolate

50g good-quality bitter chocolate,
   such as Valhrona Grand Caraque
80g unsalted butter, softened + extra
   for the trays
175g light soft brown sugar
1 egg

Butter several baking trays. Sift together the flour, cocoa powder, bicarbonate of soda and salt. Melt the two chocolates together in a bowl set over a pan of gently simmering water, then leave to cool.

Using a heavy-duty electric mixer, cream the butter with the sugar, whisking at high speed until pale and creamy. Slowly add the egg and beat until combined. Fold in the sifted flour and cocoa mixture, then fold in the melted chocolate. Cover and leave the dough to rest in the fridge for 1 hour.

Preheat the oven to 180°C, Gas 4. Roll the dough into egg-sized pieces between your palms and place on the prepared baking trays, leaving space for them to spread as they cook. Press them down slightly with your fingers to flatten. Bake for 15–20 minutes or until the edges are firm, but the centre still gives a little to the touch. Leave on the trays for a minute, then transfer the biscuits to a wire rack to cool completely.

If the biscuits are not to be eaten straight away, store them in an airtight tin or cookie jar for up to 5 days.

With an exquisitely crisp exterior and a contrasting soft, chewy centre and made from a blend of the finest dark and bitter chocolates, these elegant biscuits crunch when bitten, then melt in the mouth.

biscuits and cookies

Chocolate chip cookies

ILLUSTRATED ON PREVIOUS PAGES

MAKES ABOUT 30 COOKIES

160g unsalted butter, softened + extra
    for the trays
85g light soft brown sugar
85g caster sugar
2 eggs
400g plain flour

$^1/_2$ tsp bicarbonate of soda
$^1/_2$ tsp baking powder
$^1/_4$ tsp Maldon salt, ground fine
200g semi-sweet chocolate pieces, or
    200g good-quality bittersweet
    chocolate, cut into small chunks

Butter two baking trays. Preheat the oven to 180°C, Gas 4. In the bowl of a heavy-duty electric mixer fitted with the whisk, cream the butter with the sugars until light and fluffy. Beat in the eggs, one at a time. Sift together the flour, bicarbonate of soda, baking powder and salt, then fold into the mixture, followed by the chocolate pieces, using a spatula. You will have a stiff dough.

Roll walnut-sized pieces of dough between your palms and put them on the buttered baking trays, leaving space in between the cookies to allow room for spreading. Bake for 15–20 minutes or until the edges are firm but the centre still has some give to the gentle press of a finger.

Remove and leave to cool on the trays for a minute before transferring to a wire rack to cool to room temperature. Eat immediately or store in an airtight tin or cookie jar for up to 5 days.

The chocolate chip cookie was created by accident in 1933. Ruth Wakefield of Massachusetts added chocolate chips to a cookie mixture, assuming they would melt and merge during baking to produce a uniform result. Instead the pieces kept moistly intact and the chocolate chip cookie was born.

Lemon butter cookies

MAKES 30–36 COOKIES

115g caster sugar
grated zest of 2 lemons
115g unsalted butter, cut into
   2cm dice
3 egg whites

115g plain flour, sifted
1/2 tsp vanilla essence
1 tbsp lemon juice
1/4 tsp Maldon salt, ground fine
butter and flour for the trays

Blitz the sugar and lemon zest briefly in a food processor, until just combined, which should take about 30 seconds. Scrape down the sides and whiz for another 30 seconds. Scrape again, then add the butter and work until creamy – a few seconds.

With the processor at full speed, add the egg whites through the feeder tube. Continuing to process, add the flour a spoonful at a time. When it is all incorporated, add the vanilla essence, lemon juice and salt, and work to a thick batter. Transfer to a mixing bowl and beat for a minute with a wooden spoon. Cover the top with cling film and leave to rest for 20 minutes.

Preheat the oven to 190°C, Gas 5. Butter two baking trays and dust lightly with flour. Drop heaped teaspoonfuls of batter on the prepared trays, trying to place 15–18 equidistantly on each tray and leaving the maximum amount of space between each blob to allow for spreading. Bake in the centre of the oven for about 10 minutes or until the edges of the cookies start to brown. If you can't fit both trays on the same shelf, bake in two batches.

Transfer the cookies to a wire rack with a spatula to cool.

The pronounced lemon flavour balances the butter richness to perfection in these beautiful amber discs, which bake to a golden crisp at the rim.

Pecan butter cookies

ILLUSTRATED ON PREVIOUS PAGES

MAKES ABOUT 30 COOKIES

350g plain flour
pinch of Maldon salt, ground fine
300g unsalted butter, softened

60g caster sugar
140g pecan nuts, coarsely chopped
icing sugar for dusting

Preheat the oven to 180°C, Gas 4. Line two baking trays with non-stick baking parchment.

Sift together the flour and salt. Cream the butter with the sugar until light in colour and texture. Beat in the chopped pecans, then fold in the flour.

Roll walnut-sized pieces of dough between your palms and put them on the prepared baking trays, leaving space between the cookies to allow for expansion as they cook. Flatten them a little with your fingers. Bake for 15–20 minutes or until firm but still with some give to the gentle press of a finger.

Cool on the baking trays for a few minutes before transferring to a wire rack. Toss in icing sugar while still warm.

Butter really is the defining ingredient in these cookies, and its quality makes all the difference to the flavour. Seek out a really good Normandy butter if you possibly can.

Gingerbread cookies

MAKES 20–30 COOKIES

350g plain flour
pinch of Maldon salt, ground fine
2 tsp baking powder
2 tsp ground ginger
100g butter

175g soft brown sugar
115g dark treacle
1 egg
flour for dusting
butter for the trays

Sift the flour, salt, baking powder and ginger together into a bowl and rub in the butter, using your fingertips, until the mixture resembles crumbs. Stir in the sugar and make a well in the middle.

In another bowl, beat the treacle and egg together until evenly blended. Pour the mixture into the dry ingredients and mix to a smooth dough. Cover and chill in the refrigerator for 2 hours.

Preheat the oven to 180°C, Gas 4. Lightly butter two baking trays. Divide the dough in half and roll out one portion at a time to a 5mm thickness. Using cookie cutters, cut out shapes of your choice and place on the prepared baking trays, leaving space between to allow room for spreading. Bake in the centre of the oven for 8–10 minutes or until firm, but still with some give if pressed lightly with a finger. If you can't fit both trays on the same shelf, bake in two batches.

Leave the cookies on the baking trays for a few minutes to firm up before transferring to a wire rack to cool.

For children, use gingerbread men cutters to shape the cookies and decorate them with currants to represent eyes before you bake them.

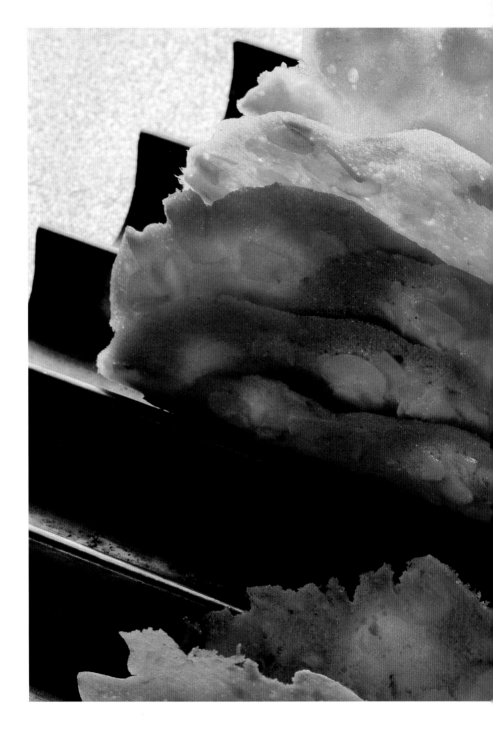

biscuits and cookies

Almond tuiles

ILLUSTRATED ON PREVIOUS PAGES

MAKES ABOUT 30 TUILES

150g blanched almonds, slivered or
chopped
150g caster sugar
60g plain flour
1 egg, separated + 1–2 egg whites
40g unsalted butter, melted

Preheat the oven to 180°C, Gas 4. Line a baking tray with a silicone
mat or non-stick baking parchment.

In a bowl, mix together the almonds, sugar and flour. Add the egg
yolk, stirring it in, then 2 of the egg whites to form a stiff batter that
should fall thickly off the spoon. If too thick, add the remaining egg
white, a little at a time. Stir in the melted butter.

Spoon 2 tsp of the mixture on to the prepared baking tray and
spread out into a 10cm circle using a fork dipped in cold water. Make
another three circles on the tray, then bake for 5–10 minutes or until
the edges of the biscuits have turned brown.

Immediately lift the biscuits off the tray with a fish slice or palette
knife and drape over a long, thin rolling pin. The biscuits will harden
almost at once into curved tuiles (roof-tile shapes), which you can
then slide off. Alternatively, place the biscuits over upturned
tumblers, pulling down the edges gently to produce cups. Continue
baking and shaping the biscuits until all the mixture is used up.

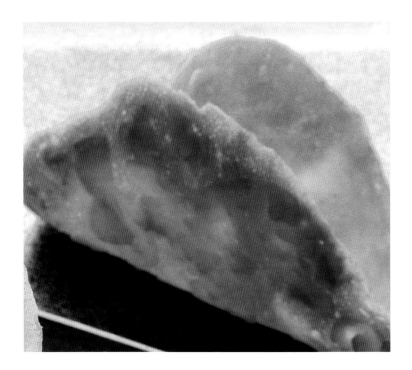

Tuiles are pliant when hot, so if you set them over a mould they retain that shape when they firm up during cooling. This makes them ideal as edible containers or, if you roll them around a cylinder, to fill like brandy snaps. They are also delicious – brittle enough to snap on the first bite, with a pleasingly chewy finish.

biscuits and cookies

Parmesan biscuits

MAKES 40–50 BISCUITS

335g plain flour, + extra for dusting
300g Parmesan, freshly grated
300g unsalted butter, chilled and diced
$^1/_3$ tsp cayenne pepper
1 $^1/_2$ tsp Maldon salt, ground fine
1 tsp coarsely ground black pepper
1–2 tbsp cold bottled spring water

TO FINISH

2 tbsp sesame seeds
2 tbsp black onion seed (nigella)
1 egg, lightly beaten

Put the flour, freshly grated Parmesan and chilled diced butter in a food processor with the cayenne, salt and black pepper. Whiz to a crumb, then slowly add the cold water through the feeder tube until the dough forms into a ball.

Scrape out on to a lightly floured surface and roll into a cylinder. You will cut the biscuits from this, so size the roll accordingly. Cling-wrap tightly and refrigerate for at least 4 hours or overnight.

Mix the sesame and black onion seeds together and scatter on a board. Brush the cylinder of dough with beaten egg and roll in the seeds to coat all over. Wrap and chill for a further hour.

Preheat the oven to 180°C, Gas 4. Cut the cylinder into 5mm slices and lay these on non-stick baking trays, leaving at least 2cm space around them. Bake for 20–25 minutes or until golden brown. Transfer to a wire rack to cool.

The ultimate, rich cheese biscuit, these make the perfect accompaniment to any aperitif and go particularly well with dry sherry. You can substitute a good mature farmhouse Cheddar for the Parmesan if you prefer.

"Pastry-making is a skill that really does improve with repetition. You learn about getting it perfect by doing it over and over. Enjoy your work. Allow it to become a pleasure, and it will soon feel effortless. Remember that the best pastry is defined by the indulgence it encourages."

DAN LEPARD

Pastries

The origin of pastry can be traced as far back as Roman times. Today, pastry describes a multitude of different forms, from a basic shortcrust for tart shells through ever more buttery variations, to arrive at perfect puff pastry and, its ultimate and complex expression, the croissant. Pastry also includes hot water crusts – robust lard-based constructions for stand-alone pies – and choux, the least pastry-like pastry, a pipeable soft paste made elastic with eggs.

pastries

Making pastry

The kitchen is not a laboratory, but comes closest to a scientific environment when we make pastry where precision is essential. With most cooking, we can make guesses based on experience. Pastry does not lend itself to such random modification, though everybody adapts and changes recipes. When these changes work, the minor adjustments they represent may be seen as incremental improvements, but do not look for revolutionary new methods. They do not exist. The first rule of pastry-making is to have an accurate set of scales and always to use them.

Pastry, particularly when cold butter is being added, does not react well to heat which is why in restaurants and bakeries the pastry-making is kept as far away from the ovens as possible. You too should always work in as cool an environment as is feasible. A marble sheet for pastry-making is the perfect cold work surface, and can be bought from a kitchen shop. It is preferable, but not essential.

Sweet pastry

MAKES TWO 25CM TART CASES

500g plain flour, + extra for dusting
150g caster sugar
100g ground almonds
380g unsalted butter, chilled and diced
    into small cubes

1 egg + 2 egg yolks
$1/2$ tsp grated lemon zest
1 tsp rum or brandy
pinch of Maldon salt, ground fine

Put the flour, sugar and almonds into a food processor and whiz at full speed for a few seconds. Add the butter dice and work again until just blended in. The mixture will resemble fine breadcrumbs. Add the whole egg and yolks, the lemon zest, rum or brandy and a minute pinch of salt, and work again briefly until the pastry balls.

Scrape out on to a sheet of cling film and either shape into a rough ball or roll into a cylinder about 5cm in diameter. Wrap and chill for at least 2 hours. Because of its high fat content this pastry can be kept in the fridge for a week, and it freezes well.

The amount of butter makes it difficult to roll out this pastry, so it is best to do this between two sheets of non-stick baking parchment. Divide the pastry in half.

For each tart case, on a lightly floured surface, roll out one portion of pastry to a round, about 5cm larger than the top of a 25cm detachable-based tart tin. Peel off the top sheet of baking parchment, then carefully pick the pastry up on the bottom sheet of parchment and lay the pastry over the tin, paper side up. Gently peel off the paper as you lift and ease the pastry down the sides to fit, taking care not to leave any air between the pastry and the tin.

If the pastry has been rolled thin, fold the overhanging pastry back over to give a double thickness around the edges. Squeeze this between finger and thumb to amalgamate, making sure that the top of the pastry is just above the height of the sides of the tin, as the pastry will shrink back during cooking.

Alternatively, cut thin discs from the cylinder of pastry and overlap them slightly to cover the bottom and sides of the tart tin, pushing down to make a coherent shell. Take care to press into the corner where the sides and base meet so there is no air between the tin and the pastry. Make the edges slightly more solid than the base and push the pastry slightly above the sides of the tin.

To bake blind, preheat the oven to 190°C, Gas 5. Line the pastry case with a sheet of foil and fill with ceramic or dried beans. (The ceramic beans have the advantage of not making the unpleasant smell dried beans do on re-use.) Bake for 15 minutes. Remove the foil and weights. Reduce the oven setting to 150°C, Gas 2. Return the pastry case to the oven to bake for another 15 minutes for the base to finish cooking to a uniform pale golden brown.

This pastry takes only seconds to make in a food processor, so it is a good idea to prepare two tart cases at the same time. One can be frozen, and then baked blind straight from the freezer without the need for a foil lining and weights, so you can have a pastry case instantly to hand.

Lemon tarts

MAKES 10 INDIVIDUAL TARTS

1 recipe sweet pastry (page 102)
8 eggs
35g cornflour
finely grated zest and juice of
    4 lemons
235g caster sugar

225g unsalted butter, cut into
    small dice

DECORATION (OPTIONAL)
good-quality bittersweet chocolate,
    melted

Preheat the oven to 170°C, Gas 3. Roll out the pastry (or cut out discs) and use to line ten 8–10cm diameter fluted tart tins with detachable bases. Prick the pastry cases with a fork (there is no need for a foil lining and weights). Bake blind for 20 minutes or until set and pale golden brown. Set aside to cool.

Lightly whisk together the eggs and cornflour in a bowl. Put the lemon zest and juice and the sugar in a large heavy-based saucepan and bring to the boil. Remove the pan from the heat. Whisk a little of the lemon-sugar mixture into the eggs, then whisk this mixture back into the remaining lemon mix in the pan.

Return to a low to medium heat and bring to a simmer. Cook for 1 minute, whisking constantly, then take off the heat. Add the butter a few pieces at a time, whisking quickly after each addition. Transfer to a wide bowl, cover the surface with cling film and leave to cool.

Put the lemon filling into a piping bag fitted with a 1.5cm plain tube. Pipe into the baked tart cases, swirling it up into a peak. If you like, decorate with a swirled drizzle of melted chocolate.

These elegant tartlets are deliciously rich, owing to the generous quantity of butter in the filling, but they have a wonderfully delicate lemony flavour.

Lemon curd tart

MAKES A 25CM TART
8 eggs
60g unsalted butter
grated zest and juice of 6 lemons
225g caster sugar
25cm sweet pastry tart case
    (page 102), baked blind

Whisk the eggs together in a bowl. In a heavy-based saucepan, melt
the butter over a low heat. Add the eggs, lemon zest and juice and the
sugar. Cook gently, stirring from time to time. When the mixture
starts to thicken, stir constantly until a thick curd custard is formed.

   Pour and spoon into the baked tart case and leave to cool and set
before serving.

Lemon curd makes a very good tart and has the benefit of
being pretty much foolproof in its preparation. The finish is
quite sharp and those with a sweet tooth may want to add
a further 60g of sugar to the curd mixture. Unless organic,
lemons are usually wax-coated and will have been treated
with chemicals, so always scrub them in soapy water, then
rinse and dry before using.

Chocolate tart

MAKES A 25CM TART

220g best-quality bittersweet
   chocolate, chopped
180g unsalted butter
6 eggs
280g caster sugar

85g plain flour, sifted
25cm sweet pastry tart case
   (page 102), baked blind
icing sugar for dusting

Put the chocolate into a bowl set over a pan of simmering water.
The base of the bowl should not touch the water. Stir from time to
time with a metal spoon until the chocolate has melted into a
coherent mass.

Preheat the oven to 180°C, Gas 4. Put the butter, eggs, caster
sugar and sifted flour in the bowl of a heavy-duty electric mixer fitted
with the whisk. Switch on at medium speed. Pour in the melted
chocolate and beat for 10 minutes.

Stand the baked tart case in its tin on a baking tray and fill with
the chocolate mixture. Bake for 20 minutes. Transfer to a wire rack
and leave to cool until warm.

Dust with icing sugar and serve with thick pouring cream.

**Rich and dark, this delectable tart is best eaten when the
filling is warm but not hot. The better the chocolate, the
better the tart.**

Chocolate and caramel tart

MAKES A 25CM TART

225g caster sugar
100ml cold bottled spring water
150ml single cream
115g unsalted butter, cut into dice
25cm sweet pastry tart case
   (page 102), baked blind

CHOCOLATE TOPPING

170g good-quality bittersweet
   chocolate, chopped
30g unsalted butter, cut into dice

Put the sugar and water in a heavy-based saucepan and bring to the boil. Lower the heat and use a thermometer to take the caramel to 180°C, when it will be a deep golden brown. Remove the pan from the heat and gradually add the cream – start with a spoonful at a time because the mixture will foam up when the cold cream hits the incandescent toffee. When all the cream has been incorporated, gradually stir in the butter to give a smooth, creamy sauce. Pour into the baked tart case and leave to set.

Put the chocolate in a bowl set over barely simmering water. When melted, remove from the heat and beat in the butter. Spread over the set caramel using a plastic spatula, then swirl the surface attractively with a skewer. Leave to cool completely before serving.

The flavours of chocolate and caramel contrast perfectly, balancing bitterness and sweetness on the tongue. The combination is rich and satisfying, nicely offset by the crisp crunch of the short pastry.

"Good ingredients are the foundation for excellent pastry-making. Take the finest you can find – the butter from your table, good dark chocolate, the cream you would serve with the ripest strawberries – and search for the right flour, soft and unbleached. Never, economise on flour as its quality will enhance the flavour of everything you mix with it. Try to work in the morning, when the kitchen is cooler, and be methodical, weighing and mixing with a swift and careful hand."

DAN LEPARD

Butter puff pastry

BUTTER PASTE
340g unsalted butter, softened
150g French T550 flour or plain flour

ASSEMBLY
560g French T550 flour, or 280g plain
    flour and 280g strong bread flour
    + extra for sprinkling
4 egg yolks
180ml bottled spring water
2 tsp Maldon salt, ground fine

First prepare the butter paste: put the butter and flour in the bowl of a heavy-duty electric mixer fitted with the paddle. Mix on the slowest speed until combined. Transfer the butter paste to a sheet of cling film and shape into a rectangle about 6mm thick. Wrap in the cling film and keep in a cool place (but not in the refrigerator) while you make the dough.

Put the flour, egg yolks, water and salt in a bowl and mix to a dough. If necessary, add another teaspoonful or two of water, but be careful – the dough will soften on resting. What you want is a smooth, but fairly tight dough. Transfer to a lightly floured surface and knead for 10 minutes or until the dough is very smooth and elastic. Shape into a ball, wrap in cling film and leave to rest for 1 hour or, ideally, overnight.

Lightly flour the work surface and roll out the dough into a rough square about 8mm thick. Place the rectangle of butter paste in the centre and fold the corners of the dough over the top to cover the paste completely (1, 2). Wrap in cling film and rest in the fridge for 30 minutes.

Place the dough on a lightly floured surface. Roll the dough out, rolling away from you, into a long rectangle about 65–70 x 35–40cm and 1cm thick (3, 4).

continued overleaf...

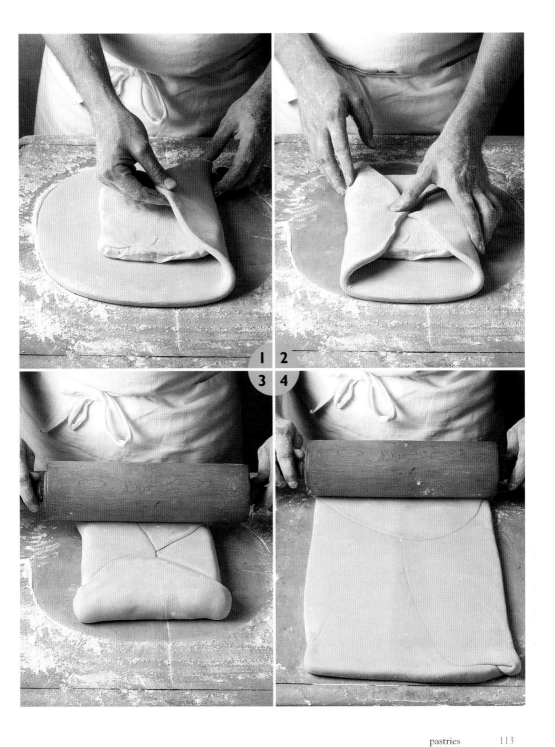

Fold one end in by a sixth and then the other end in by a sixth (5). Fold both ends over again by a sixth so that they meet in the centre (6). Now fold the two together, as if you are closing a book (7).

Next turn the dough so the fold is to one side. Roll it out gently away from you again into a long rectangle about the same length as before. Fold one end of the dough in by one-third (8), then the other end in by a third, over the top of the first third. This is a single turn.

Spread a sheet of cling film over a tray, place the dough on top and cover tightly with cling film. Leave in the refrigerator or a cool place for 1 hour.

Set the dough on a floured work surface so the fold is to one side. Roll out into a rectangle again and give it a single turn, followed immediately by another single turn. Wrap in cling film and leave in the refrigerator overnight before using.

Puff is the ultimate pastry – a buttery, multi-layered flaky pastry with each layer as thin, crisp and fragile as the next, the whole made light by the air that separates them. The skill in making puff pastry is to interleave the butter and air into the flour as it forms a dough by rolling, turning and chilling, without overworking the dough. Too much rolling and stretching produces elasticity, which in pastry results in shrinkage. The chilling is also vital. If the butter softens it will become oily and seep through the flour. Making puff pastry is not easy, although perhaps more time-consuming than really difficult. But, of course, like anything technique-based, it gets better the more you make it.

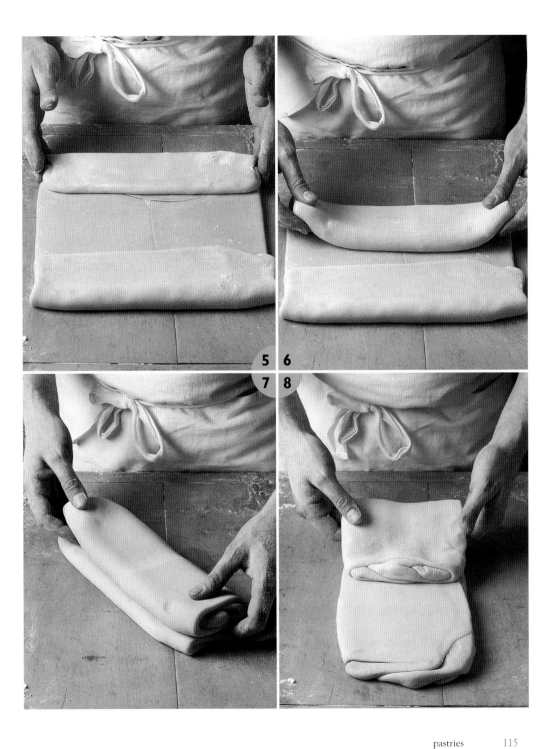

5 6
7 8

Cheese straws

MAKES 20–25 STRAWS
400g butter puff pastry (page 112)
85g Parmesan or farmhouse Cheddar,
  freshly grated
black pepper
1 tbsp sesame seeds (optional)
flour for dusting

GLAZE
1 egg yolk
1 tbsp milk

Preheat the oven to 180°C, Gas 4. Line two baking trays with non-stick baking parchment.

Roll out the pastry on a lightly floured surface to a neat rectangle about 4mm thick. Distribute the grated cheese evenly on half the pastry and grind black pepper over all. Fold the other half of the pastry over, pressing down gently. Cut across in 5mm strips, then, holding the ends, twist each strip to make a spiral shape.

Beat the egg yolk and milk together in a bowl. Brush the cheese straws with the glaze and shake the sesame seeds over, if liked. Lay the straws on the baking trays. Bake for 20–25 minutes or until puffed and golden brown. Remove to a wire rack and cool before serving.

Traditional cheese straws are dense and very rich. Good-quality puff pastry provides an effortless opportunity to create a much lighter variation on the theme. These are delicious, yet quick and easy to make.

To vary the flavour, include different spices with the cheese, giving a prickle of heat with chilli flakes or taking this one step further by scattering on finely shredded fresh chillies. Add paprika for a smoky contrast or shredded spring onions or shallots to cut the richness of the cheese. Alternatively, Dijon mustard could be spread thinly on the pastry before adding the cheese. For a different effect, instead of sprinkling sesame seeds on top, substitute onion seeds or cumin seeds.

Tarte fine aux pommes

ILLUSTRATED ON PREVIOUS PAGES

MAKES 4 INDIVIDUAL TARTS

400g butter puff pastry (page 112)

4 tbsp pastry cream (see chestnut
mille feuilles, page 122)

4 Granny Smith apples

1 tbsp sugar

2 tbsp apricot jam

flour for dusting

GLAZE

1 egg yolk

1 tbsp milk

TO FINISH

icing sugar for dusting

Preheat the oven to 200°C, Gas 6. Line a baking tray with non-stick baking parchment or a silicone mat. Divide the pastry into four and roll out each portion on a lightly floured surface into a thin round, about 15cm in diameter. Place on the baking tray. Scrape the pastry cream over the pastry with a palette knife to coat thinly.

Cut the apples into quarters and remove the cores, but leave the skins on. Slice the quarters into paper-thin slices and fan these out on the pastry discs, with each new slice slightly overlapping the last. Leave a 1cm rim of pastry uncovered. For the glaze, lightly beat the egg yolk with the milk, then brush over the pastry rim. Sprinkle the apples with the sugar.

Bake for 15 minutes, then lower the oven setting to 150°C, Gas 2 and bake for a further 5 minutes. The apples will have taken on a golden glaze while the pastry will have puffed up around the rim.

Warm the jam in a small pan until melted. Press it through a sieve to remove any large pieces of fruit, then brush over the warm tarts. Dust with icing sugar to serve.

This is an absolutely classic tart. To be exceptional this tart is wholly dependent on the quality of the pastry used. Those who choose not to attempt to make their own puff pastry are in good company, and you can now buy good frozen butter puff pastry (puff pastry made with vegetable oil or lard is only acceptable in savoury dishes). It is important to use apples that hold their shape well on baking, such as Granny Smiths. We dust the apples with a spoonful of sugar just before the tarts go in the oven and then add more gloss with a jam glaze after baking.

Chestnut mille feuilles

ILLUSTRATED ON PAGES 118–9

SERVES 8

400g butter puff pastry (page 112)	**PASTRY CREAM**
150g chestnuts in syrup, well	50g caster sugar
drained	2 egg yolks
2 tbsp icing sugar + extra for dusting	25g cornflour
1 vanilla pod	1 vanilla pod
300ml double cream	250ml milk
flour for dusting	25g unsalted butter

First make the pastry cream. Whisk the sugar, egg yolks and cornflour together in a bowl. Split open the vanilla pod over a plate and scrape out the seeds. Put the pod and seeds into a heavy-based saucepan with the milk and slowly bring to the boil. Remove from the heat and whisk one-third of the hot milk into the egg mix. Quickly tip the egg mix into the milk pan, whisking as you do so. Return the pan to the heat and bring back to the boil, stirring constantly. Boil for 1 minute. Pass through a sieve into a bowl, add the butter and stir until melted. When the pastry cream has cooled to warm, cover the surface with cling film and leave to cool completely.

Preheat the oven to 180°C, Gas 4. Line a baking tray with non-stick baking parchment or a silicone mat.

Roll out the pastry on a lightly floured surface to a 30cm square, about 5mm thick. Lay the pastry square on the baking tray. Put a wire cooling rack on top of the pastry and bake for 25–30 minutes or until the pastry is crisp and brown. Carefully turn the baking tray over so the pastry rests on the wire rack and leave to cool in a warm dry place.

Put the drained chestnuts in a food processor and pulse-chop briefly to a rough paste. Add 300ml of the pastry cream (any left over can be used as a tart or éclair filling, or topped with fruit for a simple pudding). Sweeten with about 1 tbsp sifted icing sugar, or to taste. Split the vanilla pod and scrape the seeds into the mixture. Fold together, then cover and chill for 20–30 minutes.

Lightly whip the cream with the remaining 1 tbsp of icing sugar to soft peaks. Fold one-third of the cream through the chestnut mixture.

Carefully transfer the pastry square to a board and trim the edges with a sharp knife, then cut into three equal strips. (Alternatively, if you prefer to make individual mille feuilles, cut the pastry into 24 even-sized rectangles.)

Spread one strip of pastry with the chestnut custard, then lay a second strip on top. Spread the remaining whipped cream over this and finish with the final layer of pastry. With a palette knife remove any excess filling from the pastry, and dust the top of the mille feuilles with icing sugar. For a decorative finish, score lines in the sugar with a hot skewer.

Mille feuilles – literally a thousand leaves – is nothing more than three slices of baked puff pastry layered with whipped cream and fruit or, as here, with a rich chestnut cream. The success of everything you do with puff pastry is determined by its quality. You could make a very pretty-looking mille feuilles with shop-bought puff pastry, but butter puff gives a superior tasting result.

Weighting the pastry during baking by placing a wire rack on top compensates for any unevenness in the rolling which can result in an uneven rise. The rack does not stop the pastry rising, but it does ensure a flat surface. It is not, however, essential.

Pear tarte renversée

ILLUSTRATED ON PREVIOUS PAGES

MAKES A 23CM TART

7–8 Comice pears
juice of ¹/2 lemon
500g butter puff pastry (page 112)
flour for dusting

CARAMEL

250g caster sugar
150g unsalted butter
50ml bottled spring water

Make the caramel: in a saucepan over a low to medium heat, warm the sugar, butter and water, stirring to dissolve the sugar, then bring to the boil. Reduce the heat and cook until you have a dark caramel, on the reddish side of brown. Carefully pour the caramel into a 23cm cake tin and tilt to cover the bottom evenly. Leave to cool while you prepare the fruit.

Preheat the oven to 190°C, Gas 5. Peel the pears, cut in half and remove the core. Put the halves in a bowl and toss with the lemon juice to prevent discoloration.

Roll out the pastry on a lightly floured surface to the thickness of a £1 coin. Using a plate 27–28cm in diameter as a guide, cut out a circle. Fold the circle of pastry in half and then fold again to make a quarter. Arrange the pear halves in the tin, cut side up, packing them closely together in a fan shape and filling all gaps. Lay the folded pastry over one-quarter of the tin and unfold to cover the fruit, tucking the edges of the pastry inside the rim of the tin.

Bake for 35–40 minutes or until the pastry is well risen and golden brown. Remove from the oven to a wire rack and leave to cool for 5–10 minutes.

Cover the top of the tin with a large flat plate, leaving a small gap at one side. Tilt to pour off any excess caramelly juices into a bowl; reserve these. Then, holding the plate and tin firmly together, invert the two. Sit the plate on a flat surface and lift the tin away from the tart. Cut into wedges and serve warm with whipped cream and the reserved caramelised juices.

For a tarte Tatin, peeled and segmented apples are baked in caramel with a pastry lid on top; this becomes the base when the cooked tart is inverted for serving. When such a tart is made with any other fruit, such as the pears here, it should properly be called a tarte renversée, which means upside-down tart. The buttery caramel and fruit juices soak into the pastry when the tart is turned upside down, so it is at its best served warm, though not straight from the oven because the caramel would be too hot.

Cooks develop their own little tricks to ensure a perfect result. At Baker & Spice we make the caramel first, then pour it into the mould and leave it to cool. The pears cook slowly as the caramel melts and mixes with the fruit juices, making it less likely that the caramel will burn. Use pears that are just ripe but still firm.

Plum tart

MAKES A 25CM TART

12 slightly under-ripe Victoria plums
225g butter puff pastry (page 112)
4 tbsp apricot jam
melted butter for the tin
flour for dusting

HAZELNUT FRANGIPANE
200g unsalted butter, softened
150g caster sugar
125g ground almonds
125g ground hazelnuts
100g plain flour
3 eggs

First make the frangipane: in the bowl of a heavy-duty electric mixer fitted with the whisk, beat the butter with the sugar at high speed until light and fluffy – about 8 minutes. Add the ground nuts and flour, and beat briefly. Add the eggs, one at a time, whisking to combine. Set aside.

Preheat the oven to 190°C, Gas 5. Cut the plums in half, discarding the stones, then cut each half in half and put to one side. Brush a 25cm detachable-based round tart tin with melted butter.

Roll out the pastry on a lightly floured surface into a thin round. Using a rolling pin, transfer the pastry into the prepared tin and press in gently to line the bottom and sides. Fold the edges over to give thicker sides to the pastry case, then roll gently but firmly over the top of the tin with the rolling pin to cut through the pastry and give a neat rim.

Spread the hazelnut frangipane in the pastry case, then set the plum quarters into the frangipane so that they stand upright – that is, cut faces vertical. Bake for 15 minutes, then lower the oven setting to 150°C, Gas 2 and bake for a further 35–40 minutes, when the frangipane will have risen up around the plums and set.

Remove from the oven to a wire rack and cool a little before lifting the tart out of the tin. Warm the jam in a small pan until melted. Press it through a sieve to remove any large pieces of fruit, then brush over the warm tart to glaze.

pastries

Pithiviers

ILLUSTRATED ON PREVIOUS PAGES

SERVES 8–10

500g butter puff pastry (page 112)
flour for dusting

ALMOND CREAM

250g ground almonds
250g caster sugar
250g unsalted butter, softened
2 eggs
50g plain flour

GLAZE

2 egg yolks
1 tbsp milk

Line a 20cm springform cake tin with cling film. To make the almond cream, place the almonds, sugar and butter in a food processor, and blend until smooth and the butter is thoroughly incorporated. Add the eggs and flour, and blend again for a moment to combine. Transfer the mixture to the prepared tin and spread evenly. Cover and chill until firm.

Divide the puff pastry into two pieces, two-thirds and one-third. Roll out the smaller piece of dough on a lightly floured surface into a rough round, about 25cm diameter and 6mm thick. Place on a small baking tray lined with non-stick baking parchment or a silicone mat.

For the glaze, lightly beat the egg yolks with the milk. Take the almond cream out of the fridge and turn out of the tin. Centre it on the circle of pastry. Brush around the exposed pastry edge with some of the egg glaze. Roll out the remaining larger piece of pastry to a circle 6mm thick and lay it carefully over the almond filling. Starting at the centre, begin to press and smooth the pastry out, sealing it close to the almond cream and the base circle of pastry. Be careful not to capture any air bubbles underneath the pastry. If you do, lightly prick them with a pin. Now seal around the edges with a fork, pressing firmly down to seal the two circles together.

Take a round bowl or dish that will enclose the filled part of the shaped pastry snugly inside. Press the bowl firmly down over the top so that the edge of the bowl indents lightly into the pastry edge. Remove the bowl, then cover the pithiviers with cling film and refrigerate for 1 hour.

Brush the surface of the pithiviers with egg glaze. Let this dry for 5–10 minutes. Now take a small sharp knife and trim around the edge of the pastry, leaving a 3cm border. Cut a scalloped edge on the border, if you like. Very lightly score through the domed top of the pastry, drawing curved lines that radiate out from the centre to the bottom of the dome. Finally, cut a small hole in the centre of the dome, so that any air created as the pithiviers bakes will be released. Refrigerate, uncovered, until the oven is at temperature.

Preheat the oven to 180°C, Gas 4. Bake the pithiviers in the oven for 15 minutes, then lower the oven setting to 150°C, Gas 2 and bake for a further 35–40 minutes or until risen and golden brown, and a skewer inserted through the hole in the centre comes out clean. Carefully transfer the cooked pastry to a wire rack and leave to cool.

Serve warm with a little lightly whipped double cream.

The pithiviers is a classic of French pâtisserie. Make and bake it ahead of time – though it isn't complicated, you need to give yourself time and space to work in a cool kitchen, when the house is quiet and you can concentrate on perfecting the finish.

Croissants

MAKES 16 CROISSANTS

1 sachet fast-action yeast

500g strong white flour + extra for sprinkling

110ml warm bottled spring water (20°C)

110ml cold milk (10°C)

20g Maldon salt, ground fine

70g caster sugar

250g unsalted butter

GLAZE

1 egg yolk

1 tbsp milk

Make a sponge: in a bowl, whisk together the yeast, 100g of the flour and the warm water. Cover the bowl with cling film and leave in a warm place for 2 hours, or until the sponge has risen by at least one-third and is clearly active, with lots of bubbles.

Put the remaining flour, the milk, salt and sugar in the bowl of a heavy-duty electric mixer fitted with the dough hook and add the sponge. Switch on at the lowest speed and work for 2 minutes. Turn up the speed slightly and work for 6 minutes, when the dough will be soft and sticky and coming away from the sides of the bowl. Put the dough in a polythene bag and leave overnight in the fridge.

The next day, put a sheet of cling film on the table and dredge with flour. Lay the butter, which should be firm but not hard from the fridge, on top. (If too soft you will not be able to control it.) Sprinkle a little flour on to the butter and, with a rolling pin, knock it out into a rectangle about 1cm thick. Wrap in the cling film and leave in a cool spot (or return to the fridge for a few minutes if the room is hot).

Take the dough from the bag, place on a floured surface and knock back with the rolling pin. Scatter more flour on the dough and on the rolling pin, then roll out, turning frequently, into a rectangle about 1cm thick. Brush off any obvious flour, then put the unwrapped butter in the centre. Fold the edges of the dough over the butter so that they slightly overlap at the top and the butter is completely enclosed.

Scatter some more flour over the top. Rolling always away from you, roll the dough out into a long rectangle about 67 x 40cm. Fold one end in by one-sixth and then the other end in by one-sixth. Fold both ends over again by one-sixth so that they meet in the centre. Now fold the two together, as if you are closing a book. Turn the dough so the fold is to one side. Roll it out gently away from you again into a long rectangle about the same size as before. Fold one end of the dough in by one-quarter and then the other end in by one-quarter so they meet in the middle. Now fold the two together. Seal the edges with the rolling pin. Wrap in cling film and refrigerate for 30 minutes to 1 hour.

Make a triangular template 17.5 x 17.5 x 15cm from card or rigid plastic. Roll the dough out on a floured surface to as neat a rectangle as you can, about 75cm long, 30cm across and 4mm thick. Trim to give straight edges, then cut into two pieces lengthways. Using the template, mark out and cut 8 triangles from each piece of dough.

Lay the triangles, one at a time, on the lightly floured surface with the narrow point away from you. Roll up, finishing with the point in the middle and underneath. Lay the croissants on large baking trays lined with non-stick baking parchment, leaving space round them to allow for expansion. Cover with cling film and leave in a warm place to rise until doubled in size, which should take 1–2 hours.

Preheat the oven to 200°C, Gas 6. For the glaze, whisk the egg yolk and milk together. Brush lightly on to the croissants, from the middle outwards so the glaze does not get between the dough layers. Bake in two batches in the centre of the oven for 10 minutes, when they will have expanded and started to colour. Lower the oven setting to 150°C, Gas 2 and bake for a further 20–25 minutes, or until risen and golden brown. Cool on a wire rack, making sure the croissants are not touching.

Making croissants is time-consuming and takes practice, but this is an easier method than most and produces an excellent, flaky result. Croissants are best eaten still warm from the oven. Their high butter content means that they freeze well too and can be reheated from frozen.

Danish pastries

ILLUSTRATED ON PREVIOUS PAGES

MAKES 6 PASTRIES

300g croissant dough (page 134)

a selection of fresh, canned or bottled fruit, such as peaches or nectarines, plums, apricots, apples, pears, figs or passion fruit flesh, or ready-to-eat dried fruit, such as raisins, figs, cherries, apricots and candied peel

about 150g pastry cream (see chestnut mille feuilles, page 122)

light soft brown sugar for sprinkling (optional)

3–4 tbsp apricot jam

flour for dusting

corn or sunflower oil for the tins (optional)

GLAZE

1 egg yolk

1 tbsp milk

If baking the pastries in tins, put six 8–9cm fluted tart tins on a baking tray and brush lightly with oil. Alternatively, line a large baking tray lined with non-stick baking parchment or a silicone mat.

On a floured work surface, roll the dough to a 6–7mm thickness. Using a 10cm round cutter (or a sharp knife), cut discs or squares from the dough and lay these in the tart tins. Press the dough lightly into the corners of the tins. Alternatively, shape the dough into thin ropes and coil round into 8cm circles on the baking tray. (At this point you can freeze the shaped dough for up to 1 week; thaw before rising.) Cover with cling film and leave in a warm place to rise until doubled in size, which should take 1–2 hours.

Preheat the oven to 180°C, Gas 4. If using fresh or preserved fruit, cut it into neat slices or dice, peeling as necessary. Dried fruit should be soaked briefly in hot water and then dried on a towel, unless it is very plump and moist.

For the glaze, lightly whisk the egg yolk and milk together. Spoon 1–2 tbsp of the pastry cream into the centre of each pastry case, and spread the cream with the back of the spoon to cover the base evenly.

Arrange the fruit on the pastry cream, fanning slices neatly or scattering on diced or small fruit. Sprinkle with brown sugar, if liked. Brush the exposed edges of the pastry case with the egg wash. Bake for 35–45 minutes or until the pastry is risen and golden brown.

Warm the apricot jam in a small pan until melted. Press it through a sieve to remove any large pieces of fruit, then brush over the warm pastries to glaze.

We use croissant dough for our Danish pastries because it gives a crisper and less doughy finish. The pastry can be cut into squares or rounds and baked in tins, or it can be shaped into coiled ropes. Pastry cream and fruit are traditional toppings. The baked pastries are glazed here with apricot jam, but you could also use a lemon icing (see lemon cake, page 26).

Pain au raisin

MAKES 6 PASTRIES

300g croissant dough (page 134)
250g raisins or sultanas, soaked in
    warm water for 30 minutes
1 tbsp caster sugar
$1/2$ tbsp rum
3 tbsp apricot jam
flour for dusting

GLAZE
1 egg yolk
1 tbsp milk

Line a large baking tray with non-stick baking parchment or a silicone mat. On a lightly floured surface roll out the dough to a 6–7mm thick rectangle.

Drain the soaked fruit and put it in a bowl. Add the sugar and rum and toss to coat. Spread evenly over the surface of the dough. Take one long edge of the dough rectangle and roll up like a Swiss roll, taking care none of the fruit falls out. With a sharp knife, cut this cylinder into slices 2–3cm thick. Place them on the prepared tray, with space around them. (They can now be frozen for up to a week; thaw before rising.) Cover with cling film and leave in a warm place to rise until doubled in size, which should take 1–2 hours.

Preheat the oven to 180°C, Gas 4. For the glaze, whisk the egg yolk and milk together. Brush this over the pastries. Bake for 35–45 minutes or until risen and golden brown.

Warm the apricot jam in a small pan until melted. Press it through a sieve to remove any large pieces of fruit, then brush over the warm pastries to glaze.

Pain au raisin is really a grown-up sticky bun, the dried fruit plumped in rum, the surface attractively glazed. Interestingly, during an experimental sub-contracted delivery programme at Baker & Spice, it was always the boxes of pain au raisin that became mysteriously depleted somewhere between the bakery and the customers, giving credence to the phrase, 'they are simply irresistible'.

Choux pastry

MAKES 'ONE QUANTITY'
150g plain flour
3–4 eggs
100g unsalted butter
1 tsp Maldon salt, ground fine
250ml cold bottled spring water

Sift the flour into a bowl. Have 3 eggs to hand; beat the fourth to a liquid in a bowl and reserve.

Put the butter, salt and water in a heavy-based saucepan and bring to the boil over a medium heat. As the water comes to the boil, remove the pan from the heat and shoot in the flour in one go. Immediately stir briskly with a wooden spoon until the flour and liquid are evenly combined.

Return the pan to a low heat and beat continuously for a minute, until you will have a coherent mass that comes away easily from the side of the pan. Remove from the heat and leave to cool for about 3 minutes. (If you add the eggs immediately the mixture may cook them, setting curds and ruining the mixture.)

Beat the first 3 eggs into the mixture, one at a time, making sure each egg is completely incorporated before adding the next. The mixture should be smooth and glossy. If too stiff, trickle in some of the beaten fourth egg from the bowl, beating well, and continue adding egg until the pastry looks and feels right.

Leave to cool to room temperature, then use immediately. If left too long the choux paste will stiffen so that you will not be able to pipe it or spread it easily.

Choux is a pastry oddity, being part cooked prior to baking and – with its high egg and water content – presenting as a pipeable paste. During baking the water in the paste creates steam internally, encouraging the choux to expand rapidly and set as a crisp shell with a hollow centre. This space can be filled with set custards, whipped cream or savoury mixtures.

Measuring the ingredients accurately is important, though in this recipe the precise amount of egg is deliberately not specified. You need about one egg to each 30g of flour, but eggs vary in size and flours have different absorption levels. The thing to do is beat in 3 eggs sequentially and then beat in the fourth a little at a time, stopping when the mixture holds to a spoon and only drops from it slowly. If you don't put in sufficient egg, the paste will be too dry to expand; if you add too much the mix will be too sloppy to pipe.

Éclairs

ILLUSTRATED ON PREVIOUS PAGES

MAKES 12–14 ECLAIRS

1 recipe choux paste (page 142)
pastry cream (see chestnut mille
    feuilles, page 122) or whipped
    cream for filling
butter for the baking tray

FONDANT ICING
225g caster sugar
75ml bottled spring water
2 tsp liquid glucose
corn or sunflower oil for the slab

OPTIONAL FLAVOURING
for chocolate: 15g good-quality
    bittersweet chocolate, grated, or
    cocoa powder to taste;
for coffee: 1/2 tbsp strong espresso or
    coffee essence

First make the fondant icing: put the sugar and water in a pan over a low heat and stir to dissolve the sugar. Add $\frac{1}{2}$ tsp of the glucose (or a pinch of cream of tartar), then increase the heat and bring rapidly to the boil. Boil to the soft ball stage (115°C on a sugar thermometer). Pour the mixture on to a lightly oiled marble slab and leave to cool for 3–4 minutes. (If you proceed while the sugar is too hot, the icing will go grainy.) Working with a palette knife or metal scraper, scrape under the mass, repeatedly scooping it up and over itself in a figure-of-eight movement. Continue working like this for about 10 minutes or until it becomes opaque and too stiff to lift with the knife. Then knead with your hands, pressing and folding until the icing is smooth and pliable. Form into a ball, wrap in cling film and refrigerate for at least 24 hours before using.

Preheat the oven to 200°C, Gas 6. Butter a baking tray and chill in the fridge. Heat a sharp knife or scissors in a jug of boiling water.

Put the choux paste in a large piping bag fitted with a 2cm plain nozzle. Squeeze the bag down and twist the top until the first sign of paste extrudes, then pipe out on the baking tray in 10cm lengths, cutting them with the hot knife or scissors. Leave space between the éclairs to allow for expansion.

Place the tray on the middle shelf of the oven and bake for 15 minutes until the éclairs will be well risen and have started to colour. Lower the oven setting to 160°C, Gas 2¹/₂ and bake for a further 10–15 minutes or until the éclairs are lightly browned and crisp. Remove, immediately slit open to allow any remaining steam to escape and transfer to a wire rack to cool.

Put the fondant icing in a bowl set over a pan of simmering water. As it starts to soften, add the remaining liquid glucose. If flavouring the icing, add the chocolate, cocoa, espresso or coffee essence while the fondant is being melted. Remove from the heat and continue stirring until the icing coats the back of the spoon. It should be the consistency of double cream.

Fill the éclairs with pastry cream or whipped cream, piping it into the slit. Hold each éclair upright over the bowl of fondant and spoon the icing on the top side, letting it run down to make an even layer. Leave to cool and set before serving.

Of all the choux paste creations, éclairs with their crisp, light shell, contrasting rich filling and shiny icing are the most popular. They are easy to pipe, though you'll find it easier to cut the paste cleanly as it extrudes if you use a hot knife or scissors. When the pastries come out of the oven it is important to puncture them immediately, so the steam inside does not soften the case. To be enjoyed at their best, they should be eaten soon after they are filled and iced. If you have more fondant icing than you need, it will keep well in the fridge in a covered container.

Mexican hats

ILLUSTRATED ON PAGES 144–5

MAKES 15 PAIRS OF CHOUX HATS

1 recipe choux paste (see page 142)
icing sugar for dusting
butter for the baking tray
icing sugar for dusting

FILLING

lightly whipped double cream or
   pastry cream (see chestnut mille
   feuilles, page 122)

Preheat the oven to 180°C, Gas 4. Take a large heavy baking tray (that fits in your fridge and in the oven), making sure that it is very clean, and rub generously with soft butter. Chill for 20 minutes.

Put the choux paste on the work surface next to the tray. Put a spoonful of paste on the tray and spread it with a palette knife or rubber spatula, starting at one edge, to make a rough circle about 10cm across and 4–5mm thick (1). Don't worry if it is a little uneven. The ripples made by the spatula will produce a more interesting hat. With your finger trace a neat circle in the paste, cutting cleanly through to the tray (2). Wipe any excess paste from your fingers. Spread another circle of paste on the tray, about 2cm from the first, and repeat until you have filled the tray.

Place the tray on the middle oven shelf and bake for 15 minutes, then lower the setting to 160°C, Gas 2½ and bake for a further 10–15 minutes or until the hats are puffed, lightly browned and crisp. Lift them on to a rack to cool (3). Discard the trimmings left on the tray.

Sandwich the choux hats together in pairs with the chosen filling, and dust with icing sugar before serving.

The pastry puffs and lifts off the baking sheet as it bakes, forming an unusual shape. We call them Mexican hats as they appear extravagantly brimmed, like a sombrero.

SHAPING THE HATS

Spread the choux paste on the buttered baking sheet to make discs, about 10cm in diameter and 4–5mm thick (1). Trace a neat circle just inside the edge of each circle, through to the tray (2). After baking, carefully lift the hats of the tray on to a wire rack to cool, leaving the trimmings behind (3).

Brioche dough

MAKES 'ONE QUANTITY'

1 sachet fast-action yeast
500g strong white flour + extra for
    dusting
50ml warm bottled spring water
    (about 20°C)

15g Maldon salt, ground fine
75g caster sugar
5 eggs
250g unsalted butter, softened

First make the sponge: dissolve the yeast and 25g of the flour in the warm water. Cover and leave in a warm place for 30–40 minutes or until bubbling and clearly active.

Put the remaining flour in the bowl of a heavy-duty electric mixer fitted with the paddle and add the sponge, salt, sugar and eggs. Mix at low speed until the dough comes together – about 7 minutes. Add the butter, increase the mixer speed to medium and continue to mix for about 15 minutes, when the butter will be fully incorporated and the dough will be shiny and elastic.

Transfer the dough to a lidded plastic container or cling-wrapped bowl and refrigerate overnight.

The next day, bring the dough back to room temperature and leave to prove in a warm place for 3–4 hours.

Brioche is the most luxurious of doughs, made rich and yellow with butter and eggs. This enrichment gives it a close texture, perfect to use as a spongey tart case.

Fig and brioche tart

ILLUSTRATED ON PAGES 150–1

MAKES A 22CM TART

250g brioche dough (opposite)
7–8 fresh ripe figs
60g plain low-fat bio yoghurt
60g caster sugar
60ml double cream

4 egg yolks
grated zest of $^1/_2$ lemon
scant 1 tbsp cornflour
oil for the tin

Preheat the oven to 180°C, Gas 4. Lightly oiled a 22cm fluted round tart tin that is 2.5cm deep, preferably one with a removable base. Roll the brioche dough out to a thickness of 4–5mm and use to line the tart tin. Halve the figs and place them, cut side up and slightly overlapping, on the dough.

Put all the remaining ingredients in a bowl and mix thoroughly until evenly combined. Pour this custard over and around the figs.

Bake in the oven for 15 minutes. Lower the oven setting to 150°C, Gas 2 and bake for a further 35–40 minutes or until the brioche is risen and golden brown and the filling is just set. Check after 25 minutes – if it seems to be browning too quickly, cover it with a small sheet of foil.

Leave the tart to cool to room temperature and then serve.

The amount of filling here may seem inadequate, but the brioche dough swells and rises so much it wouldn't hold a larger amount. The tart is best on the day of baking.

Glossary

allspice Aromatic brown berry the size of a large peppercorn, which is dried in the same way. In its complex aroma one can detect hints of mace, cinnamon and cloves.

baking powder This mixture of bicarbonate of soda and acid salts is a complete raising agent that only needs moisture to activate it. Also contains a large percentage of ground starch, which is included to absorb moisture from the air and prevent premature activation in the tin. It is used in conjunction with soft flour to make 'quick' breads.

beignet Deep-fried, yeasted bread dough – either a plain doughnut or a fruit fritter.

beurre manié A paste made from equal amounts of plain flour and butter.

bicarbonate of soda An alkali raising agent, also known as baking soda. When mixed with an acid, such as cream of tartar, a chemical reaction is kick-started and carbon dioxide is given off. A component of baking powder.

bran Outer husk of wheat.

brioche Sweet yeasted bread enriched with butter and egg.

Callibaut Couverture Fine high-cocoa-content chocolate with a strong bittersweet taste, ideal for making cakes and fillings for tarts.

choux (pastry) Pipeable, egg and flour paste used for making light hollow cases, such as éclairs and profiteroles.

cinnamon Dried inner bark of a tropical tree, best bought as rolls or quills of bark rather than as a ground powder, because the latter rapidly loses its flavour and fragrant aroma.

crème fraîche Rich cream with a distinctive tangy taste. It is made from double cream mixed with buttermilk heated to 75°C for several hours until it thickens and stabilises.

deflate Pressing raised dough to expel the carbon dioxide trapped as bubbles by the gluten during proving.

èclair Long choux container usually filled with whipped cream or pastry cream.

fermentation Process during which carbon dioxide is given off. This is a result of yeasts producing alcohol as a by-product of getting chemical energy from sugars.

gluten Combination of two proteins in wheat grain, which bind together when moistened, creating thin, elastic strands. These form membranes that trap the gas, causing the dough to rise.

hard flour White wheat flour with 10–14 per cent protein.

knead Working and mixing flour and water together to make a coherent, elastic and pliable dough. Kneading can either be by hand or using an electric mixer fitted with a dough hook. It encourages the gluten in flour to stretch, expand and acquire the necessary elastic properties to trap gas bubbles given off during yeast fermentation.

knock back Aggressive technique to deflate dough after initial proving.

lemon zest Thin outermost layer of the rind. Zest is used in many recipes as it contains the volatile oils that deliver the most intensely lemon flavour. Unless organic, always scrub lemons thoroughly before removing the zest because of chemicals and the coating of antifungal wax, the latter retarding oxidisation.

mace See nutmeg.

mille feuilles Multi-layered puff pastry confection. Literally 'thousand leaves', this is not an accurate description as there are really 723.

muffin Small, sweet 'quick' bread raised with bicarbonate of soda or baking powder.

muscovado Dark brown sugar produced at the first stage of refining from boiled sugar cane. It has an intense, treacly flavour. Muscovado is a Portuguese word meaning unrefined.

nutmeg Seed of the fruit of *Myristica fragrans*, a tropical tree, which originated in the Moluccas but is now cultivated in many tropical countries. The seed is covered with a reddish, fibrous membrane that separates it from the flesh of the fruit. When dried and flattened this membrane becomes mace. Mace and nutmeg smell and taste similar and are interchangeable, though mace is stronger in flavour.

oats Coarse cereal eaten in porridge, muesli and oat cakes.

organic Implies something is free of chemicals or other additives and has been grown or raised in a chemical-free environment.

palmier Sugary biscuit made from puff pastry.

pithiviers Glazed, round puff pastry pie with a rich, sweet filling. Pithiviers is traditionally scored on the top in radiating curved lines.

profiterole Small choux bun that may be filled with either sweet or savoury creams.

prove To rest kneaded dough in a warm place, during which time it rises.

rye Low-gluten cereal. When milled it produces a dark, heavy flour with a pronounced flavour.

semolina Durum wheat that is more coarsely ground than standard wheat flours.

soft flour White wheat flour with a protein content of between 6 and 10 per cent.

spring water Purified bottled still water without added chemicals.

vanilla pod Dried long, thin pod of the orchid *Vanilla planifolia*. The principal flavour resides in the seeds, though both the seeds and empty pod are used to infuse custards etc.

Viennoiserie French pâtisserie term for fine flaky pastries, such as puff pastry and croissants, in which crisp layers result from the careful incorporation of butter during repeated rolling and chilling.

wholemeal, wholewheat Flours that are darker in colour because they are made using elements of the whole wheat berry including some of the wheat germ and bran.

yeast Microscopic single-cell organism that produces alcohol and carbon dioxide as it grows, a process called fermentation. To do this it needs sugars, moisture and warmth.

Index

acknowledgments

Baker & Spice
47 Denyer Street
London SW3 2LX

020 7589 4734

www.bakerandspice.com

We have about 20 full-time staff working to create the food we make every day. Of course, this cast changes from time to time, but without the extreme hard work and dedication of our exceptional crew we would not be where we are today. The staff who have helped to create the shop we have today, listed chronologically, are:

For the bakery: David Frequelin, Remi Georgelin, DL, Amir Allon, Martin Aspinwall, Jason Warwick, Remek Sanetra, Henri Bellon de Chassy, Damon Cowan, Sally Parsons, Amar Slimani.

For the Viennoiserie: Patrick Lozach, Ram Sivaram, Martin Doak, Lionel Rocher, Ilan Schwartz, Mariangela Pratt.

For the pâtisserie: Henri Berthaud, Yannick, Amal Ibrahim, Ari Aboso, Alexandra Queruel, Yvan Cahour, Dorit Meinzer, Jeanne Hertz, Linda Osedo, Louise Riviere, Jaime Foa, Megan Jones, Mark Lazenby, Markus Herz, James Webb.

For the traiteur: Lorraine Dunne, Sammy Leopold Santos, DL, Michelle Wong, Kate Lewis, Sami Tamimi, Ruth Taylor Hunt, Pavel Kuzdak, Cayetano Lopez.

For the shop: Karen Copland, Natalie Laurent, Zoe Field, Tamsin Borlase, Anne Boyle, Fiona Kinnear, Stephane Boucton, Leonor Gomez, Laurent Beauvois, Helena Allon, Fabio Calascibetta, Alessandra Figini, Belen Mateo, Jaclyn Dove, Emma O'Reilly, Naima Ali, Anna Plym, Jenny Mellquist, Andrea Novak, Eric Ackermann, Daniel Marcolin, David Doulay, Candice Nieper, Kirsty McGregor, Amanda Hale, Anna-Marie Briers, Ari Economakis.

Kitchen assistants: Vince Mejia, Tito Bosales, Cesar Aristizabal.

For the bread factory and gail force: Amnon Mer, Pierre Corneille, Richard Vintiner, Samantha Oyez, Jackie Hobbs, Terry Stockwell, Nimal Kandihi.

Our drivers: David Ormston, Paul Stimson, Steve Bragg, Richard Fenton, Ray Mechell, Errol Palmer, Arthur Albert.

Our friends: Melanie Pini and Sophie Braimbridge (who suggested and created our first series of chef demonstrations), Naomi Kaplan (forever a source of inspiration), Anissa Helou, Peter Gordon, Jeremy Lee, Lyn Hall, Ursula Ferrigno, Giorgio Locatelli, Elizabeth Luard, Alastair Little, Juliet Peston, Heston Blumenthal, Jonathan Archer, John Kelly, Enzo Zaccharini, Honor Chapman, Sarah Standing, and the customers who have supported us from the beginning.

All our recipes have an origin, as do recipes in every cookbook. Though these recipes have been written or adapted and tested especially by Dan Lepard and Richard Whittington, the inspiration has come from friends. We are especially grateful to Dorit Meinzer for Chocolate pecan cake, Devil's food cake, Marble cake, Lemon cake, Parmesan biscuits and Chocolate chip cookies; and to Naomi Kaplan for the Plum cake and Pecan butter cookies.

For the production of this book, Baker & Spice would like to thank Divertimenti of Fulham, Kitchen Aid UK, Phillip Brittain and Solstice, Neal's Yard Dairy, Jeni Wright, Peter Howard, Coralie Bickford-Smith, Bridget Bodoano and Caroline Perkins.

We also thank Emily Andersen for the use of her photographs on pages 1, 7 (centre), 9, 11, 12–13, 14, 17 (centre), 53 (centre), 69 (centre), 97 (centre), 98–9, 110–1 and 141.

If you have difficulty obtaining any item of kitchen equipment, then Nisbets of Bath offer a mail order service (01454 855555).